BAREFOOT TO THE WHITE HOUSE

★ ★ ★

CAROLYN SUNDSETH
with Jimi Miller

Carolyn Sundseth

ISBN 1-931600-82-1

ACKNOWLEDGMENTS

My first acknowledgment goes to my Lord for His faithful watch care which enabled me to live through these experiences. I would also like to thank Youth With A Mission for teaching us the principles set forth in the Bible for hearing God's voice and answering His call. Through these teachings I have learned God does not want me to be independent but that He wants me to trust Him as my total source. Loren Cunningham's teaching on giving up our rights to ourselves has been invaluable to me on this journey. I also want to thank Victor, my husband of forty years, who has been a great househusband, prayer partner and companion during these unusual events in our golden years.

CONTENTS

Foreword 5

Preface 7

1 The Call 10

2 Preparation 24

3 Colorado Forever 37

4 Divorce 49

5 Remarriage 53

6 Turning Point 68

7 Next Door to the White House 72

8 The White House 88

9 "Reagan Aide Says..." 100

10 Not Yet, Lord? 122

11 Fired Up — and Fired 128

12 Foreign Missions 138

13 Full Circle to Go! 145

14 Ports of Call 156

15 Go for It! 166

Appendix A 171

Appendix B 173

Appendix C 176

Notes 178

FOREWORD

This is an inspiring story of a faithful, courageous woman.

I have known Carolyn for many years and have always been deeply impressed with her love for the Lord and her boldness and diligence in being a witness for Him in every available opportunity. Because of her availability to the Lord, He has placed her in some amazing circumstances, even very high places of government. They have not been easy circumstances, but in God's great wisdom, you can see why He chose Carolyn instead of someone else. Readers will find her story thoroughly fascinating.

This book is a testimony of God's faithfulness and presence, even in the midst of storms. It is also an expression of what can happen when one person takes seriously God's command to be obedient, commits her heart to Him and allows herself to be used for His purposes.

God's kingdom is enhanced, and the world is better off, because there is a Carolyn Sundseth who said, "Here am I, Lord. Send me."

Bill Bright
President and Founder
Campus Crusade for Christ International
April 1992

PREFACE

Commit to the Lord whatever you do, and your plans will succeed. The Lord works out everything for his own ends.
Proverbs 16:3-4a, NIV

In his heart a man plans his course, but the Lord determines his steps.
Proverbs 16:9, NIV

One benefit of aging is to look back at how God uses everything — even our wrong decisions — to prepare us for service. He not only uses everything, but He also knows how He will even before we are born. As it says in the Psalms, "All the days ordained for me were written in your book before one of them came to be" (Ps. 139:16, NIV).

In December 1980, when God Himself became the delight of my life, His plans for me became the desire of my heart — to serve Him through Youth With A Mission's maritime relief division, known as Mercy Ships. But, like Abraham on Mount Moriah, I first had to be made willing to sacrifice the vision to Him before He could fulfill the desire (Gen. 22:1-14; Ps. 37:4-5).

Made willing!

To prepare me for the fulfillment of the vision, God-ever-patient bypassed my treacherous self-sufficiency to demonstrate my deep need for His unfailing all-sufficiency. He then led me away from what I thought I wanted to do at the moment, through a career in the White House in Washington, D.C. Then followed a couple of more detours, until He could use me where He had planned all along. He never left me. In spite of qualms and misgivings on my part, not once did He ever abandon me (Heb. 13:5c).

For years I knew Jesus as Savior of my soul but did not understand Him as Lord. I was busy doing things for Him instead of getting to know Him intimately. I became more efficient (and complacent) in my job and my busy work in home, church and community, all of which combined to produce a self-sufficient, self-directed, independent me.

Independence, of course, is a virtue ranking right up front with motherhood and the work ethic as a most-favored American trait. Isn't it? God didn't seem to think so. He called me out of my comfort zone of independence.

With our move to Hawaii my life-style changed dramatically. From being an efficient executive secretary in a large corporation, I became a Jill-of-all-trades in our own small contracting firm. Confidence in my ability to handle any situation disintegrated.

Through my frustrations God-ever-present was teaching me His principles of interdependence on others and total dependence on Him.

I remember meditating on Abraham's willingness to sacrifice his only son, Isaac, while at the same time trusting in God's promise to make him the father of many nations through that son (Gen. 17:3,4,16, NIV). God helped me understand a spiritual truth my accumulated skills and successes had obscured: Even as Abraham and Isaac left the servants and started up to the altar of sacrifice, the thicket was rooted in place, and the ram was coming up the mountain.

God-who-loves-me had the solutions to my dilemmas in place or on the way before I asked (Matt. 6:8).

My story is written on these pages to encourage Christians like me who sometimes — or often — find themselves in places of confusion and delayed fulfillment of desire.

Fellow sojourner, take heart! Stop, look and listen! Regardless of your natural abilities, talents, education, wealth or lacks thereof, regardless of your age — answer God's call on your life. The burden to supply what you will need to accomplish that call is His, not yours. He only desires our complete obedience and trust in Him.

God-ever-mindful has a thicket in place and a ram coming up the mountain for you.

Carolyn Sundseth
Van, Texas
January 1992

ONE

The Call

A man's mind plans his way,
but the Lord directs his steps and makes them sure.
Proverbs 16:9, AMP

December 1981

For Vic and me life was a quandary. Home building in the islands was all but dead. Our construction business in Kailua-Kona, Hawaii, hardly supported the staff and us not at all. I hadn't written myself a paycheck in more than eight months.

Vic had partially retired in 1980 after a miraculous cure from colon cancer, and we had been working toward his full retirement and our full-time missionary service with Youth With A Mission — life, limb and livelihood at the Lord's disposal. But now it looked as if we would have to close the door and sell our happy, hospitable home just to make ends meet.

Six years earlier, shortly after we had moved to

Kona from Colorado, YWAM transferred their international headquarters lock, stock and barrel from Switzerland to Kona and became our near neighbors. The YWAM leaders chose Kona by direct guidance from God to concentrate their major evangelistic thrust toward the unreached peoples in the Pacific Basin.[1] (Youth With A Mission workers often abbreviate the name of the organization to YWAM, which is pronounced y-wam.)

They bought the old Pacific Empress Hotel, occupied at the time by transient humans and island critters. By hand and bulldozer they freed her from impacted nests and weeds, dressed her wounds, clothed her with fresh new paint, restored and refurbished her with love, and adopted her as their home base.

Because Vic and I owned a local contracting company and paint store, we soon became well acquainted with the industrious YWAMers and their leaders, sharing our common faith in the Lord Jesus Christ.

In 1978 YWAM bought the M/V *Anastasis*, a world-class, ocean-going vessel, from Greek merchants and outfitted her for worldwide mercy ministry. Infatuated with the ship, my heart's desire became to sail with her wherever she might run to the cry of the world's desperate and dying. Vic's heart was emphatically not so inclined. YWAM, yes. *Anastasis*, no. At a hopeless impasse, we were, nevertheless, both convinced we were hearing from God to serve Him together in foreign missions and that we were to prepare for it.

Our initial step in preparing for service, wherever God might send us, was to attend YWAM's Crossroads Discipleship Training School for forty-some-things. (Our boys call it Codger-roads Discipleship Training School.) We had spent from January to April 1981 in the training school.

The second and probably final step would be attending the counseling school that would take place from January to April 1982. Having applied early we were sacrificially "casting all our care upon him" (1 Pet. 5:7) by arranging to sell all our material encumbrances — house, painting franchise, paint store and contracting business.

On December 10 we received a letter from YWAM, which I was sure would be confirming our acceptance. I opened it and scanned the first few lines.

"Vic," I cried, "I don't believe this! YWAM rejected us!"

Vic looked up slowly from his tinkering and said after a pause, "I didn't think YWAM rejected anybody."

"Especially not those who do as much for them as we do!" I complained. Prayers and intercession! Physical labor! Support checks! Hospitality on call! All three sons in the ministry! And didn't we faithfully occupy two old, cold, rusty, metal folding chairs every Friday night at their jam-packed, open-air meetings at the base?

I wondered whether to blame our rejection on Vic's slow-talking, deliberate ways or on my trigger-happy motor mouth.

I felt disappointment in the leaders who were supposed to pray us into their schools, disappointment in God who was supposed to give us the desires of our hearts (as He promised in Psalm 37:4-5).

Vic read the letter over my shoulder then said, "No, Lyn, you didn't read it all. We haven't been rejected by YWAM, just from starting counseling school this January. They suggest we reapply for the April school."

April! I felt scuttled. "April is months away," I complained. (Fretting was one of the things I did best.) "What about our plans!?" (Our plans included unloading the business on someone who could make it pay before we had to declare bankruptcy.)

Our situation was slipping out of control. I hoped it didn't sound as if I were accusing Vic of anything, but with an exorbitant twenty-one percent interest rate almost no one on our island was building houses. And, as in any other small, family-owned business in such an economic climate, the owners of the business (in this instance, Vic and I) were the only ones not getting regular paychecks.

Vic said, "It's all right, Lyn. We're not ready. I can't retire in two days. We still have too much to do to sell the house and close out the business. Besides, you have a lot of bookkeeping to catch up on along with all the other things you do in your so-called spare time." He chuckled quietly to himself.

All the other things included frantically juggling Bible studies and prayer meetings, keeping house, running the office, mixing paint, keeping books, climbing ladders, delivering drywall, surrogate-mothering some of the young Pilgrims, attending Christian Women's Club and serving a term as president of the Women's Aglow Fellowship on the island.

Vic was right — we weren't ready. I really did need time to sort out, catch up and regroup. And God was reminding me of something I had copied from my devotional by Oswald Chambers: "It is easy to imagine that we will get to a place where we are complete and ready, but preparation is not suddenly accomplished; it is a process steadily maintained...it is preparation *and* preparation."[2]

The phone, as was its custom every few minutes, rang. The caller was Holly Coors, wife of my Colorado-based, long-term, former boss, Joe Coors. Holly was calling from Washington, D.C.

After joyful greetings she said, "I'm serving on President Reagan's transition team, and they still haven't fully staffed some of the top jobs at the agencies. Are you willing to come to Washington to be a glorified secretary at the Pentagon?"

Secretary, to me, meant dozens of carbon copies of everything.

"Holly," I said, "I have no desire to be stuck behind a desk as somebody's secretary. Running our construction business and paint store office has been secretarial enough for me. Besides, I also have no desire to return to Washington. Vic and I plan to be traveling foreign missionaries for God, and we're going to counseling school. [Someday, I thought to myself.] No, thanks, Holly. Thanks, but no thanks!"

Not one to close a door, Holly said, "Well, if you change your mind, let me know."

I assured her I would not change my mind. Little did I realize that the ice was cracked, and a seed had been dropped into the soil.

Six weeks later, on Friday, February 12, I dashed home from work, whipped off my faded, functional muumuu and pulled a newer, fancier one over my head. I was already pushing the clock and didn't want to be late picking up our guest from Australia for the Christian Women's Club luncheon.

Trying in vain to ignore a ringing telephone, I finally gave in and grabbed the receiver off the hook.

"Hello, this is Carolyn," I said.

The voice said, "One moment, please, for Morton Blackwell from the White House."

I had neither seen nor heard from Morton since 1976 when I had worked at an agency in Washington, D.C. Since then President Reagan had appointed him special assistant in the Office of Public Liaison. One part of his duties was to be the liaison for all religions (including strange cults) except Jewish and Roman Catholic, which had their own liaison officers.

"Carolyn!" he greeted me as if it hadn't been more than five years. "How are you?"

Something was up. He wasn't calling me from the White House to ask how I was doing. He probably wanted the phone number of a Coors family member or a chunk of time out of my life to rally support for some cause he was involved in. Either would have been fine. I was glad to hear from him.

"I'm fine, Morton. How are you?"

"I'm calling to see if you are willing to come to Washington as my confidential assistant."

"Confidential assistant?"

"Fancy name for executive secretary. Nobody comes to Washington to be a secretary except a cabinet member."

"Why me? I don't even own a pair of shoes. How did you find me here?"

"Why you? Because who else adept at politicking has as obstinate a Christian witness as you do? How did I find you? Let's just say somebody slipped me a note."

"I don't know, Morton. I really don't want to be in Washington, and I really don't want to be a secretary." (The words had a familiar ring.)

"But this time you would be working in the OEOB (Washington jargon for the old executive office building) and the White House, much nicer than at the agencies: no cheap conservation on heat and air conditioning like in the Carter administration; long hours maybe, but great perks: nice office, meetings with the president, better pay...."

"How much?"

"Very healthy starting salary between $35,000 and $40,000. How does that sound?"

I said, "Well, none of that will be the deciding factor. If the Lord wants me to serve Him there, I'd be willing to scrub toilets for God and country."

"We could add that to the job description."

"No, thanks, Morton. By the way, do you realize I'm fifty-nine years old?"

"Not an item."

(Should I tell him I'm also forty pounds heavier than when he last saw me? I decided against it.)

"I don't know, Morton," I said. "Vic and I believe God is calling us into foreign missions, and I'm not sure D.C. qualifies."

"You'd be surprised."

"I do promise that we'll pray about it, and I'll call you back as soon as we have an answer. Is that fair enough?"

"Carolyn, there are good, conservative Republicans pounding the gates to get in here to work for Ronald Reagan. But, in your case, fair enough. I'll be waiting to hear from you."

When the phone clicked off on the other end, I stared at the receiver in my hand. I was stunned. Yes, I wanted to go on the mission field — anywhere — but to Washington, D.C.? The only place I wanted to go to less than to Washington was to YWAM's Hollywood base where the main ministry was to nine-year-old prostitutes. Holly's call was one thing but a

16

summons to the White House? Quite another.

I had to talk to someone.

I phoned Vic, but he was out on a construction site somewhere. After pacing for a minute, I decided not to tell anyone until I first discussed it with him. Still, I was about to burst.

Vic, where are you!?

I slapped on some lipstick and drove over to pick up my guest from Australia. As soon as she was seated in the car I blurted out, "Guess what! I've been invited to work at the White House!"

I could tell how utterly impressed she was by her blank stare. Then she pricked my bubble by asking, "What's the White House?"

The Christian Women's Club in Kona met in the King Kamehameha Hotel, a popular tourist attraction on Kailua Bay. As an extension of an elegant shopping mall, the "King Kam" sits next to the bustling, boat-jammed pier which hosts the annual International Billfish Tournament. And its torch-lined, public beach cove is the site from where the Ironman triathletes are launched on the first leg of their all-day October races. I had trouble finding a place to park.

Mary, my best long-time friend and prayer partner, was seated at the head table with the club officers. As my guest and I slipped in unobtrusively but late behind them, I leaned over Mary's shoulder and whispered, "I've just been invited to serve on the White House staff. PRAY FOR ME!"

She stared open-mouthed while we found seats at a table nearby. I heard nothing during the entire meeting except a drumming through my brain: WHAT will I wear? What WILL I wear? What will I WEAR?

At home later that day when I told Vic about Morton's call, he made little comment. We quietly discussed the pros and cons of moving to D.C. Then we prayed about it briefly and went to bed, and he went to sleep.

I lay in bed wide awake, praying. I got up and went outside on the lanai (the Hawaiian word for porch). Across the water I could almost make out the shadowy contours of Maui and Molokai. I counted the lights of the many fishing boats anchored quietly out in the ocean and the few lights of our little, somnolent Keahole Airport down at the water's edge. I prayed, went back to bed, then prayed some more.

I thought about our business, Kana Kamalii, created to help the Pilgrim converts develop a useful, temporal life along with eternal life in Christ.

With some of the Pilgrims helping, Vic and I had remodeled an old warehouse into our offices, paint store and storage. Then, following Hawaii's strict building code, we constructed lava-rock walls around feathery hapu ferns with their notches supporting cymbidium orchids and planters overflowing with brilliant-red, mainland geraniums, their gnarly clumps rarities among the exotic, tropical blossoms.

(Lord, is it "Bloom where we're planted," or "Onward, Christian soldiers"?)

With no apparent answer from the Lord, Morton's phone call became as amorphous as a dream.

Saturday morning broke bright and clear. Vic left early with Gale to repair a school roof in Naalehu on the south side of the island. I was left alone in my beautiful Palisades home with one of the most momentous decisions I would ever have to make:

whether to leave Kona for some other reason than to join YWAM. If foreign missions were not to be the end result, Kona, Hawaii, would be a very hard place to leave.

Wrestling with my choices, I did not know that Vic and Gale were praying together off and on all day and that before they returned home they both had God's assurance that this was His call on our lives. But I knew very well that during my own praying and pleading for guidance, God was reminding me over and over that "to obey is better than sacrifice" (1 Sam. 15:22).

Vic and I were eager to obey, but what was He saying for us to do?

All day my imagination was cornered by the supreme argument of why I could not go: I had nothing suitable to wear.

I had stretched-out bathing suits expanded to their limits but no nice suits.

I had voluminous muumuus but no dresses for formal occasions. The perennial not-so-funny joke about muumuus is that, if you wear them enough, pretty soon they fit.

I had bras but no slips. I had a thin rain slicker but no winter coat. Fins for my feet but no gloves for my hands. A snorkel mask but no hat. Nothing toward a basic wardrobe for a job of such status.

I had rubber-soled flip-flops — "slippahs" to the Hawaiians — and one old pair of gold sandals but no heels and no snow boots. And besides after seven barefoot and semi-barefoot years, I wasn't sure I could ever again walk in real shoes.

Meanwhile, I kept creating visions of myself standing before a three-way mirror making my *poi* figure look trim in fitted, mainland clothes. (*Poi* is a famous Hawaiian dish made from the taro root. Its fame comes from its calories as well as its taste.)

A second argument: woefully insufficient funds. What about rent? What about transportation costs? With only Vic's Social Security check to supplement my base salary, how were we to live in expensive Washington.

Battling to keep my mind focused on God's desires and His will, I finally faced the truth: In spite of years of churchgoing and religious good works, I was no spiritual giant.

I called Mary. "I can't go! I know God provides and that He is my source, but I have never before faced having to depend on Him completely."

"I remember many times when you and Vic prayed in enough money to cover your payroll and taxes and insurance payments," Mary replied. "Hasn't God always been faithful?"

"But, Mary, could the Creator of the world really care whether I have the proper clothes?"

"If He cares how many hairs are on your head, He surely cares about what you put on your body. Remember, He dresses the lilies of the field, and He made fur coats for Adam and Eve. How do you know they weren't chinchilla or mink?"

"But, Mary, knowing God's principles in your head and living by them from the heart are two different issues. And another thing: I'm totally out of touch with what's going on in Washington, and I can't believe this call to the White House has anything to do with my ability to advance the causes of the Reagan administration."

"Maybe God's going to give you a crash course in 'learning to lean.' "

"But, Mary, do you have any idea how traumatic

such a move could be for us?"

"Nope, can't say that I do."

"Well, do you understand how our life-styles will have to change?"

"Of course! No geckoes, no cane spiders, no mongooses, no Kona cruisers...." (Hawaii's Kona cruisers are one-inch to two and a half-inch long flying cockroaches.)

"No sun tan, no snorkeling, no beaches, no volcanoes, no parking places...."

"But, Carolyn — senators! Congressmen! Briefcases! Subways! Soot! Traffic! Live news on TV! Crime! High heels!"

"Do you think I should accept?"

"I'll pray for you."

And I knew she would lift me up to the Lord in prayer until the answer came.

The answer came later that same day. During a time of quiet devotion with the Lord part of a verse from the book of Esther in the Old Testament seemed to come alive on the page: "And who knows but that you have come to the kingdom for such a time as this and for this very occasion?" (Esth. 4:14c, AMP).

My decision was made. I would go. It was further confirmed when Vic and Gale came home, then confirmed again by the prayers and prophetic words of Roy Ishihara and David Rees-Thomas, two pastors in Kona.

When I later submitted the idea to Loren Cunningham, YWAM's founder and president, he said, "It's about time we sent someone to those folks. We've been praying for them for a long time."

Monday, February 13, was Presidents' Day, a legal holiday. When I called Morton back on Tuesday to confirm my coming to Washington, I was told that he had waited by the phone all day Monday for my answering call. I had assumed incorrectly that all the patriots at the White House would be celebrating Presidents' Day someplace else.

I asked for time to prepare, and we agreed that I should appear in Washington ready to work on April Fool's Day.

During the ensuing six weeks I continued to rationalize why I should not go. Even if I had the money to buy clothes, I had been to the mainland only three times in seven years and had no idea what the working women were wearing. Worse still, after a lifetime of achievement through my own efforts, when I compared myself with others on the president's staff, I was suddenly overwhelmed with the knowledge that I was totally inadequate. Perhaps it was God's mercy that kept me from reading on in Esther to the end of verse 16: "If I perish, I perish" (Esth. 4:16d). Instead, He-who-comforts comforted me with this truth: "God is not impressed with the positions that men hold and He is not partial and recognizes no external distinctions" (Gal. 2:6b, AMP).

Even so, many times I was on the verge of calling the White House to confess I had made a terrible mistake in agreeing to go.

Vic applied and was accepted to YWAM's counseling school without me. He would join me in Washington in July. Meanwhile, he needed me to help close down the business while I was still in Kona.

One of my assignments was to drive up to the Hawaii state offices in Kealakekua to close out our workmen's compensation and unemployment insurance files.

Becoming impressed with my weighty new position, I explained to the young local clerk there that I was closing our business to work at the White House.

She snickered at my announcement and gave me a strange, rather rude overhaul with her eyes.

On my way home I stopped by to report her baffling reaction to our Hawaiian church secretary who burst out laughing. She explained that in Kealakekua the White House (no longer in business) had been a house of ill repute. The clerk evidently thought I had been hired to resurrect it.

Far from rejecting us for going to Washington, the YWAM leaders gathered all the Protestant ministers on our side of the island together for a love feast on their regular fast day when they pray for our nation and its leaders.

After the meal, they gathered around, first to pray for Vic, then to pray for me. Asking God to protect me and to anoint me with wisdom and discernment, they commissioned me by the laying on of their hands as their missionary to the White House. I was deeply moved. Catching a glimpse of Gale's big grin on the front row, I let the tears flow. Later I thought of the verse that says, "For not from the east nor from the west nor from the south come promotion...but God...lifts up" (Ps. 75:6-7, AMP).

Now that I was committed and commissioned, friends sent farewell cards with bills and checks tucked inside. When the time came to leave the island, I had gifts totalling more than a thousand dollars, the first time I ever had that amount to spend on clothes and other personal needs — the assurance I needed that my heavenly Father had known all along what I needed, which was, among other things, something to wear.

TWO

PREPARATION

When my father and my mother forsake me,
then the Lord will take me up.
Psalm 27:10

I will instruct thee and teach thee
in the way which thou shalt go:
I will guide thee with mine eye.
Psalm 32:8

February 1930

Harrison, Arkansas. Population, approximately five thousand.

In 1930 poverty was the rule rather than the exception. My hometown, Harrison, Arkansas, neighbor to Dogpatch, U.S.A., was nestled in the heart of the Ozark Mountains and struggled with the rest of the nation in deep economic depression.

In the cities fathers and bums strung out their bait on their fishing lines (gum on a string) to catch the occasional errant coin winking up at them from under a sewer grid. Harrison had no sewer system. As a matter of record, few Arkansas houses had either electricity or indoor plumbing except right in the towns. We lived on a farm.

My daddy, Carl Hamilton Brown Sr., was an accountant with a small railroad line. He and Uncle Hubert also owned and ran a dairy, processing their milk with a big, loud, secondhand, dark yellow Delco generator. With the combined income the depression didn't affect us as much as it did many others in the Ozarks. When Daddy's salary at the railroad was cut, at least he still had another one coming in, and we raised much of our own food.

My memories seem to begin one day in the spring of 1930. I was seven; my brother, C.H. Jr., was six; and our older sister, Ernestine, was in school. C.H. and I were in town at Aunt Mary's house, playing outside with the children next door. I wore Ernestine's hand-me-down, plaid wool coat with a bulky sweater under it that squeezed my arms. A metal clasp holding my hair bow in place under my knit cap was poking my head, and the tail to the cap was around my neck like a scarf. I had no gloves, and my hands were cold. My much-mended, long, white, cotton stockings had new holes but not so many as C.H.'s brown, cuffed, knee socks and corduroy knickers. C.H.'s hair stuck out like twigs from under his cap.

Aunt Mary, in a cotton house dress and silk stockings rolled down to just below her knees, stood in the front door and called, "C.H.! Carolyn! Come in the house and sit down. We have something to tell you."

The "something" was that Mother had "gone home to be with the Lord." When Aunt Mary said that, something invisible hit me in the stomach and something inside me grew cold like a cramp. C.H. and I sat quietly side-by-side on a little slipper rocker until C.H. finally said, "Can we go play now?"

With permission granted we went back out to our waiting playmates, and C.H. said, "Mama's gone to be with the Lord."

"Where's that?" asked one of the kids.

"Up there someplace," said C.H., pointing to the sky.

"When did she go?"

"Just now, I suppose," he said.

"How did she do that?"

"On a cloud, I guess. Maybe we can see her go by." And we four sat silent and still on the cold front steps, carefully searching each flying cloud to watch for Mother floating by high over the dusty houses and vacant lots on her way to heaven. I thought maybe I was supposed to cry, but C.H. didn't, so neither did I. I wondered why I didn't.

I vaguely remember riding to primary school crowded into the rumble seat of our model-A Ford among cold, wobbly milk cans; of eating Sunday dinners at different restaurants each week to help the owners pay on their milk bills; of us three kids tormenting a series of somber and unsuspecting housekeepers.

I clearly remember trying to tell Daddy something when he offered me a nickel to shut up for five minutes; climbing up behind C.H. on our Shetland pony, Prince, with doll and pajamas tucked under my sweater; and holding tight around C.H.'s waist and staring at the back of his neck while we trotted through the shadowy backwoods to Grandma Travis's old, drafty, rambling farmhouse. I recall Daddy's bringing home his new bride, Lorene, a girl from a neighboring farm who was eleven years younger than he, and thirteen-year-old Ernestine's leaving shortly thereafter to board at the School of the Ozarks about forty-five miles from home. The school had been founded by Presbyterians in the early twentieth century and provided a four-year high-school education for young men and women from remote areas not served by the county school buses.

Daddy and Lorene were very much in love and made it plain that they preferred us kids not to be at home. Even though Daddy seldom remembered our birthdays, he carried a card with Lorene's glove size, hose size, silver pattern and favorite scents and often brought home gifts for her on special occasions — or just because. I thought they were very romantic.

My girlfriend's father owned a diner where she and I worked after school for no salary selling hamburgers and bowls of chili for five cents apiece. It was then that I decided I wanted to be a waitress for my life's work.

Meanwhile I worked diligently to complete the memory work for communicants in our Presbyterian church. Confirmed at twelve, I set the goal for myself to read the Bible through. By the time I met Jesus in the Gospels, I had developed a personal relationship of sorts with Him, though not quite understanding which one of us was supposed to be in charge of my life.

In the fall of 1935, the same year that Ernestine graduated, I enrolled in the School of the Ozarks.

Prayer and work assignments were survival measures for the school. All students attended Bible study and prayer meetings daily and worked at least sixteen hours a week.

Students and staff prayed daily for enough coal to run the power and heating system. Students also quarried stone, did electrical and plumbing installations on new buildings, ran the print shop, the heating plant, the dining room, the kitchen, the laundry and the dairy. Students also maintained a large farm and canning factory where they grew, harvested and canned most of their food. Clothes came from big-city churches in the Midwest into our boutique which we called by its real identity, the Charity Room. Occasional gifts of money came to the school from various sources. But prayer and work were the order of the day.

When Daddy and Lorene drove me to the school, I was both eager and anxious, not feeling quite grown up enough to be leaving home, but excited at the idea of all-new clothes and lots of new friends. Little did I realize how socially unprepared I was or how adept and quick I would be to accumulate the demerits that would translate into hours and hours of extra work. It was a good thing I liked to work!

The campus spread out across a beautiful bluff overlooking the White River. The buildings were bare, somber blocks of dark red brick with huge, dusty windows. But the familiar sights and smells of dairy and farm life that surrounded the bleak buildings set me at ease.

The high-ceilinged dorm rooms were bleak and cold, but the students were friendly. In a room for four freshman girls I was assigned a top bunk, one small closet and a wooden chest with two drawers.

After Daddy and Lorene took my things to the room they seemed bored and eager to leave, so we said good-bye. During my four years there they visited several times, but from that first day they seemed to remove themselves into the background of my life.

Lights out in the dorm came at nine o'clock, with a five-minute advance warning of flashing lights.

During my first week I got caught in the shower

when the lights flashed. With no time to rinse off, dry, dress and get into bed by deadline, I waited until I was sure inspection was over. Then, with my nightgown bunched in my arms, I dashed naked through the darkened hall straight into the beam of the startled housemother's flashlight.

She shrieked. Ten demerits!

I soon led a few cohorts into harmless pranks. We got on a roll short-sheeting beds, propping half-full buckets of water over half-open doors, rolling metal wastebaskets down the uncarpeted stairs at midnight, catching frogs and dropping them down the necks of seniors' dresses in the lunch line.

"I can't believe you and Ernestine Brown come from the same family!" the housemother would storm. "She was such a lady!"

Eventually, the momentum caught up with us, and we went too far.

In cahoots with two others, I retrieved a dead mouse from its trap. Then, choosing the most squeamish girl on the hall, I shoved it deep down into her bed.

That night we waited for her scream. No scream. The next morning we waited for her to say something. She said nothing. We wondered what she was up to, what revenge she might be plotting.

We wondered for almost three days, then the stench of the dead mouse caught up with us. I had mistakenly stuffed the stiff little corpse not between the sheets but between the bottom sheet and mattress cover. Until it began to stink, our victim had not known it was there. We had to evacuate the dorm.

President Good capped off our mouse escapade with a chapel talk in the auditorium about some medical students playing a practical joke using a human corpse and frightening the victim out of her mind — permanently.

That cured us. Never intending to hurt anyone, we swore off practical jokes and settled down to serious study. Attending the school was a wonderful opportunity, and we didn't want to be expelled.

After having declared my career objective to be a waitress, by the end of the second week I found my job assignment — serving three meals a day — hard work and boring. I requested a change and was immediately reassigned to work in President Good's office. I went with high hopes and expectations.

President Good decided that after two weeks in the classroom practicing shorthand I should be able to take dictation. He, therefore, had me excused from the classes to work those extra hours for him. As a result, the brief forms and phrases everyone else learned in class I invented out of necessity. No one has ever been able to help me read my shorthand.

President Good's secretary and bookkeeper both gave me friendly hands-on instructions on how to file, reply to letters, take dictation, type materials, answer phones, work as a receptionist, and give the same quality attention to a student with a problem as to a major donor with money. And I developed a new career objective: I would be a secretary.

Meanwhile I also developed a voracious appetite for reading, especially the classics, which, according to the school librarian, I was not old enough to read.

During my senior year just on a lark I took the exam for teachers for the county schools. Only sixteen years old and with absolutely no desire to teach, I passed the test and was offered a job teaching in the two-room country school in Capps, Arkansas, where my Aunt Elma was principal.

I shudder today when I think back to how much I thought I knew at that age.

In early August 1939, two weeks before my seventeenth birthday, I started teaching school.

Aunt Elma and I had forty students, most of them dressed in patched jeans and socks but scrupulously clean, from poor, uneducated but proud families. Only a few came smelling like their pets and farm animals.

Our two-room school in Capps stood about a mile and a half from our home place in a grove of trees next to a little white church and cemetery. The boys carried water up from the spring and chopped wood for the pot-bellied stove that heated the two rooms and warmed the provisions from the county's hot lunch program sent to supplement our sack lunches from home. Two outdoor privies served the boys and girls separately.

One plump little boy's mother greeted me by saying, "Whup him, Miss Carolyn. I whupped him oncet, and he learned his alphabet right off."

I was never tempted to "whup" the kids, but we did expel a sharecropper's seventeen-year-old son, who was enrolled in the second grade, when he refused to stop smoking in the privy.

Some of my pupils were cousins I had never met; others were children from the rental houses on our property. Sometimes they brought me gifts. We played games like baseball, tag and drop-the-handkerchief at recess and at noon.

At first Aunt Elma taught the top four grades; I taught the lower four. But because I had trouble teaching the little ones to read, we traded after one month. The main thing I learned that year was that I was not a teacher and did not want to be one.

Because my father was a thirty-third degree Mason, a level few people attain, both my mother and Lorene joined the Order of the Eastern Star, a group open only to women relatives of men with at least the degree of Master Mason. Without these two groups, there would have been few social events in many small towns. So in 1940 for my eighteenth birthday Daddy arranged for my membership in the Eastern Star. It wasn't until years later that I learned the dangerous philosophies behind this organization.

I had taken a civil service test earlier that same summer. But with no response from the government by late August I enrolled for the fall term in Park College, a Presbyterian boarding school in Kansas City. The only interesting things I did there were replacing my entire wardrobe with clothes of my own choosing and attending Eastern Star meetings in nearby Ft. Leavenworth with one of Park College's faculty wives.

After only one school semester I was bored and discontent. So when the results of the civil service test came with the offer of an appointment as a clerk-steno in Washington, D.C., I accepted. Graduation from the School of the Ozarks had marked the end of my formal education in secretarial science, but I was adept in all phases of office work, and all my new clothes were well suited to a business career.

Upon my arrival in Washington, the massive, marble state buildings overwhelmed and thrilled me at the same time. I was ecstatic, confident about my future. I rented a room then sought out the Masonic Hall for "family." The hall was on New York Avenue, near the New York Avenue Presbyterian Church which I also attended while Peter Marshall was pastor, never even slightly discerning the irreconcilable differences between Masonry and Christianity.[1]

The room, which I shared with two other girls, was in an old embassy building. For fifty dollars a month each, we had breakfast and supper served to us along with about fifty other young government employees every day in a huge gold, red and mahogany dining room. A house boy notified us of our incoming phone calls and ran our fancy elevator which had red, silk brocade walls.

I reported to work on February 12, 1941 (exactly forty-one years before Morton's momentous 1982 phone call to me in Kona), at the Office of Production Management (soon renamed the War Production Board) in a building facing the mall. My handsome starting salary was $1,440 per year, comparable to about $10,000 in today's economy

One Sunday, after only one week on the job, I was assigned to check security passes at the front desk. Intensely aware of the rules pertaining to the assignment and inordinately proud of my delegated authority, I refused General Knudsen entrance when he showed up without a pass. How was I to recognize the chairman of the board of General Motors on loan to our government to head up a government agency?

General Knudsen was not amused. He demanded I call my supervisor who came and hurriedly rectified the embarrassing situation.

Humiliated, I learned three things for future reference: One, that recognizing our country's VIPs was a must. Two, that reading the daily newspapers would teach me to recognize the VIPs. Three, because government assignments are made at one's discretion, absorbing protocol as I went along would make me ready for the chips to fall where and when they would.

Investigative reporter Drew Pearson came in one day asking questions. He was trying to establish that, instead of our using shipping tonnages to get precious war commodities out of the Far East, we were using them to get bananas out of Central American republics.

I helped him all I could and was quoted as a government source the next day in his column, fortunately not by name. Seeing my words quoted in the newspaper article so intimidated me, I learned a fourth thing for future reference: that I must be very careful what I said to reporters from then on to forever.

Everyone I met drank. I came from a dry county and a Christian school, so it was all new to me.

One of my roommates, who worked for a senator, was assigned to entertain a small-town editor at a nightclub on a Saturday night. Not wanting to miss a date with her boyfriend, she asked me to go along as a blind date for the editor.

"I don't know how to drink," I said.

"Don't worry," she said. "Just order a Tom Collins. It tastes like lemonade."

I did, and it did. I drank several and do not remember leaving the night club or getting home. But the next morning when I woke up under a cold shower still fully clothed from hat to shoes, my roommate told me I had thrown up all over the editor-constituent's white suit and the senator's car.

The episode wasn't funny then, and it isn't now. But it did not deter me from pursuing the fast life while at the same time attending morning church services from habit, sometimes alone with a hangover, and evening church services with my room-mates. Maybe we went for the sermons, maybe for the free sandwiches and Cokes set out for the service-men we helped entertain.

Old habits hang on. As the Bible says, "Train up a child in the way he should go: and when he is old, he will not depart from it" (Prov. 22:6).

My Christian upbringing at home had been rein-forced by myriads of answered prayers at the School of the Ozarks. And, in spite of my chosen life-style in Washington, I prayed often — frivolously at times, perhaps. But God-who-is-faithful stood by me, keep-ing me from making permanent mistakes.

By early 1944 I was tired of being a government bureaucrat struggling with low pay and long hours. When a friend from the Republican National Com-mittee offered me a job as researcher/writer, I re-signed from the War Production Board and accepted the job which involved getting voting records out to Republican nonincumbents to help them in their campaigns. (At the time the few Republicans in Washington could have caucussed in a phone booth.)

My love affair with politics began during those days of analyzing the *Congressional Record* to glean what I could to help our Republican candidates. Nor has it diminished over the years. It changed me into a dedicated Republican and, as I learned and ma-tured, a more and more conservative Republican at that.

I am forever grateful that Daddy, who was the Democratic committee chairman in our county in Arkansas, never dropped in on me unexpectedly during those years. I needn't have worried. With no Republicans in northern Arkansas at the time, he never even told anyone who I worked for or what I was doing.

Shortly after my change in jobs, I met John Nelson, a tall, handsome (though balding), forty-year-old aide to a New Deal senator. It happened at a Thanksgiving dinner for twelve which he had prepared himself — but to which I was not invited — when a friend took me over to say hello.

In John I found someone who was as lonely as I was. He was considerate, mature and willing to love me unreservedly, to get me tickets to hearings on Capitol Hill and to teach me to cook. Even though he was twice my age, we fell in love. In June 1944 we were married and lived happily ever after — for two and a half years.

THREE

Colorado Forever

If any man has a hundred sheep,
and one of them has gone astray,
does he not leave the ninety-nine on the mountains
and go and search for the one that is straying?
Matthew 18:12-13, NAS

March 1947

U nder the combined stress of postwar politics and fast living, John suffered a near fatal heart attack. For that reason, we turned our backs on D.C. and moved to Coeur d'Alene, Idaho, to be near John's son. There John fulfilled his heart's desire by buying a house not far from a music store he already owned in town.

I settled in the house, joined the Young Republicans, found the nearest Presbyterian church, volunteered as sponsor for Job's Daughters of the Eastern Star and helped John in the store. I was content.

John told me that if I were truly happy with him, if he died I would want to marry again. I didn't believe him.

After an idyllic summer a second heart attack took John's life on October 1, leaving me at twenty-four, a grieving widow alone in a big house, suddenly responsible for a store I didn't know how to manage with full-time help from only the radio repair man, supplemented by part-time help from John's son.

The ceaseless moan of the autumn winds sweeping through the pine trees that surrounded the house sounded like the sighing of lost souls. And with the foggy, dreary lake behind the property I felt as though my life read like a gloomy, Gothic novel. When the snow came, it piled in mountains.

Christmas and the next ten months came and went unnoticed as I grieved and tried to cope alone. Finally, on a cold, dreary October day I escaped by train to visit my family in Arkansas, changing trains in Denver in unseasonably bright, clear sunshine. The temperature was 70 degrees, and there was no wind.

Back in Coeur d'Alene, I signed over the store, the house, the furniture and the car to John's son. With only a small income from some stocks I owned, I moved to Denver.

I rented a room at the Denver YWCA, bought a newspaper and scanned the help-wanted ads, looking for something more challenging than simple typing and filing. I soon landed a job as a service representative trainee with Mountain Bell Telephone Company. Before long the vice president of operations, who was slated to be promoted to president within the next few years, wanted and needed an executive secretary, someone with service representative training. Of the two hundred or so in-house service representatives in the office, only two of us qualified, and one was dating the vice president's best friend. So by default I advanced to the position, moving up to the executive floor — the youngest ever to work there — and scheduled to move right on up with my new boss into the president's office, set for life (so I thought) in a fascinating, exciting, challenging and all-consuming career.

One of the first things I did in Denver was have the diamonds from my wedding ring reset into my Eastern Star ring. I also became active in a small, conservative Presbyterian church in North Denver where I attended the couples' club alone and taught Sunday school to the youth.

Denomination headquarters had recently issued a radically new curriculum designed to make Sunday school more interesting for the liberal Presbyterian young people and to involve their parents in their Christian education. As a result, the old conservative pastor who had been there twenty-six years was forced out, and the church split.

As I overheard church members argue both sides bitterly, I realized I had never honestly analyzed what I personally believed about the inerrancy of the Bible, the virgin birth of Jesus Christ, His deity, His bodily death, resurrection and imminent return, or any other tenet of my faith — baptism and communion, for examples.

I had been a pew-sitter without contributing much of anything except Sunday attendance, token monetary donations, mental assent, routine Sunday school teaching and a few hours of volunteer casual labor in an aimless sort of way, unaware that perhaps I was simply involved in "the tradition of men, according to the elementary principles of the world, rather than according to Christ...which have, to be sure, the appearance of wisdom in self-made religion and self-abasement...but are of no value against fleshly indulgence" (Col. 2:8,23, NAS).

My conclusion was that because I gave mental assent to the Apostles' Creed, I was religious enough and no doubt headed for heaven.

After five years of widowhood I was almost twenty-nine and ready to marry again. With my newly gained head knowledge and understanding of God's kingdom, I was also ready to have children and raise them in what I conceived to be a Christian home. Unfortunately, the attractive men I met who were close to my age were either newly married or newly divorced and not interested in trying again.

Then in December 1951 I met Vic.

Kay, a friend of mine from Eastern Star, called me to say that her husband Russ's cousin, Vic Sundseth, a construction worker from Alaska, had come down to go duck and deer hunting with Russ. He also wanted to go dancing. Kay asked if I were available to go out with them on December 8 to celebrate Russ and Kay's first wedding anniversary. I was available.

Russ had told Vic that I was plump but that he would never notice it from the way I was "stacked."

Vic, suntanned, strong and energetic with thick, wavy, black hair and an impish grin, did not in the least resemble the office types I had been dating.

We met and fell madly, passionately in love.

After eight dates in eight days we began planning a big church wedding for February 15 (just two months away) with a long, romantic honeymoon to follow.

Like me, Vic had been married before. Unlike me, he had children. He also had been divorced (he thought) for two years.

I hated divorce and had strong, religious convictions against it, so I promised Vic I would never leave him — that he would be stuck with me for both life and eternity.

After our eight-day, whirlwind romance Vic left on the sixteenth to spend the Christmas holidays with his family in Everett, Washington. I followed, arriving on Christmas Eve. I met his mother and several of his surviving siblings with spouses and children, aunts, uncles, cousins, his three adopted children, his own eight-year-old son, Gale, his ex-wife, Ann, and her two babies. They all hugged and kissed and drank a lot and laughed and played poker and yelled at each other affectionately. I had never seen a family act like that. They were wonderful. But even while swarmed by his relatives, I had eyes only for Vic. We were so in love it was impossible to imagine waiting two whole months. We discussed getting married immediately.

First, though, I asked to see his divorce papers. What we learned was that Ann had never paid her share of the lawyer's fee, so the decree had never been filed.

She consented to pay, and the lawyer promised to file the papers on the first court day in January. We went ahead with our plans with confidence in the future and in our mutual promise to establish a Christian home.

Our wedding day was February 15, 1952. We honeymooned at the Grand Canyon and someday will go back to see it. It was completely hidden behind a thick cloud cover.

But Ann never got around to signing the divorce papers until the Monday after the wedding, so we weren't legally married. We would have to get married again. To avoid embarrassment we drove to Wenatchee for the license, using Vic's Anchorage address and one of my old ones from D.C. days. We were married again in April by a justice of the peace in a town near Seattle, specifically requesting that the event not be published in the newspapers.

Shortly after the second wedding, Vic's youngest son, Gale, moved in with us. We sued for custody and won, and when his school was out for the summer the three of us moved to Denver.

To capture a touch of the romance I had witnessed and envied between Daddy and Lorene, I slipped a card with my glove size, hose size, silver pattern and the scents I liked into Vic's pocket.

On my birthday in August, which was also our six-month wedding anniversary, Vic arrived home with gifts — gloves, hose, silver and perfume. No card. No gift wrap.

"What's all this?" I asked him.

"Well," he answered with innocent candor, "I found this shopping list in my pocket and I thought you wanted me to buy this stuff for you."

In late November Vic was offered a job as outfitting foreman for some minesweepers being built by the Bellingham Shipyards. My first inclination was to urge him to turn it down so we could stay in Denver. But an older, wiser woman advised me to go where Vic wanted to settle for the sake of our relationship. So I resigned from my job, and we moved to Bellingham, Washington, onto a yacht in Bellingham Bay owned by Vic's boss. I was pregnant with our son Chris at the time (and sick), and the only thing they had on board to drink was hot buttered rum. Chris was born in late June with our son Mark following in early June the next year.

In October 1959 the five of us moved from Washington "permanently" back to Colorado. Early in

1960 Vic went to work in the city of Golden for the Coors Construction Company, the largest building contractor in Colorado. I went back to work for Mountain Bell in Denver.

In 1962 the Coors Porcelain Plant, the only manufacturer of chemical porcelain in this hemisphere, offered me a place in their typing pool. Even though I was highly overqualified, I accepted to be working closer to the school the boys were attending and was soon promoted to typing pool supervisor. Eventually Vic and I bought a beautiful brick home on a cul de sac in the shadow of Table Mountain.

The Coors family-owned corporation was (and is) the most moral and ethical for which I have ever worked. The brothers, Joe and Bill, take good care of their employees, knowing most of them — about eight thousand when I worked there — by name. We were confident and secure, "set for life" — until 1964 when Vic was laid off in the Coors corporation's work-force reduction.

After sellng our home, I resigned from my job, and this time we moved to the up and coming new state of Alaska. We were sure we could find reconstruction work for Vic in the rubble of the biggest earthquake ever known to hit North America, a quake that had occurred in the area around Valdez and Anchorage and resulted in more than four hundred million dollars' worth of property damage. Not so. We were back in Denver within ten months.

Meanwhile, Coors's construction had increased dramatically, and Vic was offered his old job back. The man who had bought our house and assumed our loan went bankrupt, so we also got the house back. And I was asked to return to Coors Porcelain but this time as secretary to President Joe Coors and his two top officers. We would "stay forever."

During the summer and fall of 1965, my dormant interest in politics was revived when Joe Coors ran in the statewide election for regent of the University of Colorado. Colorado was then one of the two states whose regents were elected rather than appointed by the governor. I spent almost as much time working with the campaign staff as at my job at Coors. As a matter of fact, the entire campaign was exciting for our whole family. Not only did we hold the Young Republicans rally in our home, but all three of our young boys distributed campaign literature. Our son Chris, who now has a degree in political science, begins his political resumé when he was eleven years old, distributing literature in Joe Coors's 1965 campaign.

Joe was elected, and the six years of his tenure were not only exciting for all of us, but often scary. For instance my first taste of real violence on the political scene occurred during a seminar at the university. The speaker was S.I. Hayakawa, at the time president of San Francisco State College (later a senator from California). He was one of very few school administrators in the United States having success controlling the dissidents on his campus.

We entered the auditorium to take our reserved seats and found them occupied by Black Panthers.

In spite of his small size, President Hayakawa leaned forward over the footlights on the stage and rebuked the belligerent Panthers, who then started throwing chairs, bottles and other debris up onto the stage. When they came up on the platform to take over the microphone, someone called the police. We made a quick exit out the stage entrance into the alley and fled to the home of Professor Ed Rozek, where we listened to radio reports of the police calming down the riot and emptying the auditorium. When I remembered having stepped on the big foot of one of the Panthers with my sharp spiked heels, I was terrified.

Joe Coors has long been known as "Mr. Right Wing" in Colorado and across the nation. In the late 1960s, he was closely associated with the founding of most of the groups the press called the New Right — sometimes called the Religious Right because of their pronounced Judeo-Christian values. One of these New Right groups, the Committee for Survival of a Free Congress (now the Free Congress Foundation), was founded and headed by our future good friend, Paul Weyrich, from Wisconsin.

During Ronald Reagan's terms as both governor and president, Joe worked on his kitchen cabinet, a group of successful businessmen who served as advisors without pay. Whenever the New Right would get a coalition together to push something through Congress or stop something from going through, they would frequently call Joe (among other generous contributors) to ask for help in getting letters and phone calls through to other business leaders. Because Joe was frequently out of town, I was the one who fielded the calls and, more often than not, passed the information on to those who might be interested in helping. Thus I became as familiar with Paul Weyrich's Free Congress Foundation, Morton Blackwell's Leadership Institute, the Heritage Foundation and its forerunners, and all the conservative activists in Washington, as I was with the Colorado University people and the other manufacturers of industrial ceramics.

During this time Vic was promoted to project supervisor at Coors. Our life appeared more stable than either of us had yet experienced. Except for our ten months in Alaska our two youngest boys, Chris and Mark, had all their schooling in the same neighborhood until they went into the armed services. We were both teaching Sunday school at our local Presbyterian church where I was an ordained elder. We were enjoying our beautiful home.

Raising three boys, from any standpoint, is an all-out, all-encompassing proposition. Somewhere at some time Vic and I had read a funny story that whoever asked for a divorce had to take the kids. But with us it wasn't funny. Our love had grown cold.

Vic had what I considered a drinking problem. I tried every way I knew to deal with it: I drank with him; I stayed home and worried about him; I ignored him; I yelled and threatened. All to no avail. Finally, I got so I just went to sleep and didn't know — and tried not to care — what time he got home from bowling or golfing or hunting or wherever he was drinking with his buddies or alone.

We had bought a camper. Every weekend we loaded supplies and kids and went fishing in the mountains. In the fall Vic took the boys hunting for doves, ducks, geese, deer and elk. I attended all school and sports events — Little League, soccer and wrestling matches, teacher's meetings and more. Often, when I had a day off, I took the boys and their friends rock hunting to add to their own collections and start a rock garden in our backyard. In our hearts Vic and I were leading separate lives while trying to keep the boys from falling through the cracks.

On my part I felt I had consistently tried to tell Vic everything but that Vic had consistently told me nothing of real importance.

On his part he probably never said much to me for

fear of getting a more complicated and wordy response than he could sift through.

Somewhere along the line I decided that I was fed up and would leave him — not divorce, just leave — as soon as Mark reached eighteen years old. That would be in June 1973.

In the interim I would simply grow older working in political campaigns and serving in state and county conventions.

Gale, meanwhile, had moved to Kona on the Big Island of Hawaii and been saved through the ministry of the Fellowship of Christian Pilgrims, who were mainly evangelizing the runaways and throwaways who lived in the jungles and beaches. Gale wrote to tell us of his conversion, confessing that all the hours and days of Sunday school and church we had inflicted on him in his youth had finally borne fruit. In 1972 he invited Vic and me to Kona to celebrate our twentieth wedding anniversary. But I didn't want to go with Vic. I wanted to stay home to do what I was already scheduled to do. Vic went without me.

What I was scheduled to do was to conduct a communications workshop, the "Indiana Plan," up in the mountains west of Denver for a group of Disciples of Christ leaders. I had been trained as moderator for this plan at Ghost Ranch, the Presbyterian training school near Santa Fe, New Mexico, and I loved it.

The plan's premise was that adults were not "taught" in their churches because leaders did not "communicate" in meaningful ways.

Participants, therefore, were to choose a topic, outline it and discuss it for an hour, actively listening to the other speakers while maintaining eye contact. It was ironic that I endorsed the concept wholeheartedly yet never seemed to communicate — much less maintain eye contact — with my husband at home.

Unfortunately these church leaders could not agree on a topic for discussion. At a verbal impasse, we took an unscheduled break, and I went walking in the snow with a young man who told me an amazing story.

"I've been expelled from my denominational pulpit for speaking in tongues," he said. (See 1 Cor. 12:10 for more about this gift of the Spirit.)

"Speaking in tongues? What's that?" I had never heard such a strange phrase.

"It's one of many powerful, supernatural gifts of the Holy Spirit," he explained. "It's in the Bible. It comes with being baptized in the Holy Spirit. Another gift is called gifts of healing. I've been baptized in the Holy Spirit and, recently, when my little boy was sick with croup, I anointed him with oil, and he was immediately healed." (See Matt. 3:11 and 1 Cor. 12:1-11 and 14:1-15 for more about the baptism of the Holy Spirit and James 5:14-15 for more about healing.)

I did not believe him. In spite of my having witnessed hundreds of answered prayers at the School of the Ozarks, I did not believe in miracles. But I said, "My husband needs this baptism in the Holy Spirit, or whatever you called it. He needs a miracle in his life, especially the power to overcome his addiction to alcohol."

It did not occur to me that I, too, needed the miracle nor that this could be the beginning of the "something deeper spiritually" for which I had petitioned the Lord for years.

Nor did it occur to me that God had a thicket in place and a ram coming up the mountain for me.

FOUR

DIVORCE

We love because he first loved us.
1 John 4:19

March 1973

After Vic returned from visiting Gale in Hawaii, our local newspaper, the *Jefferson County Sentinel*, carried an invitation to a breakfast meeting at the Holiday Inn in Golden to organize a local chapter of the Full Gospel Business Men's Fellowship International. Vic decided to go, and I went with him.

The speaker was George Loving, a man we both knew slightly because our sons were friends. George told how he and his wife had recently noticed a baffling change in their eldest son's attitudes and actions.

When questioned, the boy claimed to have been "baptized in the Holy Spirit with the gift of speaking in tongues." (There were those terms again!) George also had had the experience and was now a founding officer of the Golden, Colorado, chapter of FGBMFI.

Later at home Vic said to me, "Gale prayed for me to have that, but I didn't notice any difference. I brought home some books."

"I don't notice any difference, either," I said. "What books?"

"*They Speak With Other Tongues,* by John Sherrill — he's an Episcopalian, by the way. And *The Sayings of Chairman Jesus.*"

"I've never heard of either one," I said. "Just put them on the bookshelf."

Drawn by the obvious love among the FGBMFI members, Vic attended all the subsequent meetings and went to hear every speaker who came to town. I went with him, grasping at any straw that might "change Vic." I was hardly affected by any of the testimonies, although at one meeting when the speaker was teaching on how to "linger and receive," I almost went forward. But I decided not to. Whenever anyone in the group spoke in tongues, it sounded like Hebrew to me. I decided they were imitating each other.

But Vic changed. He quit smoking immediately and cut way back on his drinking.

When I saw that the changes were apparently permanent, I privately decided that I really could leave him and not worry that he might drink himself into oblivion or set himself on fire in bed.

My father's sudden death in April reinforced my decision. I now had no one to answer to but myself.

Little did I realize that, starving as I was for "unconditional love," I was classically unwilling or unable to supply it for Vic.

One evening in May while we were in the living room reading, Vic began acting strange. His mouth began to work. He left the room abruptly, went outside and into our camper, locked the door and, I learned later, began to "speak in tongues." When he came back in, he said nothing about it to me. I probably hadn't noticed he was gone. Soon, when he could stand it no longer, he went back outside and spoke again, fluently this time in a language he did not recognize except as one of love and worship to God. Next day, same thing. And the next day.

Some weeks later, when I arrived late at our share group, Vic was telling our friends about his experience with tongues. I resented the fact that it was the first time I had heard about it, too. (Or was it the first time I had really listened to him?)

On Chris's birthday in June, when I announced to Vic that I was planning to leave him, he did not ask me to stay. It wouldn't have made any difference anyway; my heart was cold. I felt only a tremendous need for a target date to be released from a burdensome situation in which I felt we were both living a lie, unable to communicate with each other beyond a surface level. We needed to communicate at a heart level. I bought a mobile home and moved in with our son Mark on July 1. Shortly thereafter Vic quit his job, saying he planned to move to the West Coast with one of his sisters.

A lawyer remarked to me, uncharitably, that anyone who would leave a work situation two years before his retirement benefits would pay off could not be trusted in other matters. It did not occur to either of us that Vic was suffering the ultimate rejection and a broken heart and could not bear to stay in Golden where every hill, every tree — everything —

reminded him of me and our twenty-two years together.

Then, because of a complication in my father's will, the lawyer advised me to seek a divorce. Because Colorado had a no-fault divorce law, it would be simple.

I waited until January to file. That way Vic and I would have the financial advantage of filing a joint income tax return for 1973. We sold the house and, as agreed, split everything fifty-fifty. Finally, in spite of having broken my vow never to divorce Vic, when the papers were signed and filed and the twenty-seven-dollar-fee paid, I was free (I thought).

Before Vic moved, as a friendly farewell gesture, I invited them all to dinner — Vic, his sisters, his cousin Russ and Kay.

After dinner, as they were leaving, Vic said, "Well, Lyn, I may as well tell you what I think of you."

"Sure, go ahead," I answered. "Say what you want to say in front of these people. They're your relatives."

"I still love you," he said, "and if you ever want me back, just let me know."

He had not said "I love you" for years. But, as far as I was concerned, the words came too late.

FIVE

REMARRIAGE

With man this is impossible,
but with God all things are possible.
Matthew 19:26

November 1974

My friend Maxine could fly free to Hawaii. She wanted to tour Maui, Oahu, Kauai and the Big Island for twelve days in November with someone who could drive the foreign, five-speed rental cars. We had traveled together before, so she asked me and I said yes.

Shortly after our divorce, Vic had moved again from the West Coast to Kona to be near Gale. He had already visited Golden twice since the divorce, and both visits had proved unprofitable — except that now we understood that the problems we swept under the rug were not due to his drinking or our totally diverse backgrounds but from our inability to communicate. On this trip, therefore, I had neither desire nor inclination to visit Vic.

No problem. Vic lived on the Kona side of the Big Island, and our plans included the Hilo side only.

No problem, that is, until Chris phoned from his Marine base at El Toro and Mark from his Alameda Naval Air Station, both threatening never to speak to me again if I didn't make the effort. So I dropped Vic a note inviting him to meet Maxine and me for lunch at the Volcano House Restaurant on Sunday.

In the interim I read *They Speak With Other Tongues* by John Sherrill.[1] After all, if good Episcopalians like John and his wife, Elizabeth, believed in this Holy Spirit business, at least I wanted to know about it.

For our island-hopping agenda, Maxine and I agreed to entertain ourselves in the mornings, then meet for lunch before doing a sightseeing thing in the afternoons. Our plan for the Big Island was to fly into Hilo from Maui early Saturday, visit Volcanoes National Park and meet Vic for lunch as our sightseeing thing on Sunday, then fly out of Hilo to Honolulu and home on Monday.

In the airport on Maui, some lady travelers noticed my Eastern Star ring and struck up a conversation. They had just come from Kona, their favorite spot on the island circuit, and urged me to go at least to visit Gale whom I hadn't seen since he moved to the islands. The flight, the women reminded me, would only take twenty minutes.

I discussed it with Maxine who assured me she would not mind flying alone to Hilo and meeting me there later. Then I phoned Vic, and he agreed to get me a hotel room in Kona for Saturday night.

When I asked the Maui ticket agent to change my flight, he looked at my ticket and said incredulously, "You want me to do WHAT?"

54

"I want you to change my Hilo flight to Kona," I said. Couldn't he understand plain English?

He shrugged and handed me back the ticket. My flight reservation already read from Maui to Kona. I looked at Maxine's ticket. Her reservation read from Maui to Hilo. How could that be?

Maxine's ticket had been made up by her son, a United Airlines reservation supervisor. Her son then gave me a copy of her schedule, which I passed on to the Coors travel agent, who was to make my reservations to match hers.

If I had known then what I know now about God's involvement in the details of our lives, I would have known He was up to something (see Matt. 10:29-30).

In Kona I learned that the Fellowship of Christian Pilgrims ran a gift shop, gardening service, delicatessen, secondhand store, several ministry houses (the True Vine, Barnabas House and others) and other projects to help support their fellowship. Vic was already immersed in the projects and the ministry. Under the Pilgrims' sponsorship he had applied for a license to remodel and build. Meanwhile he was training some of the young converts in building skills, while serving the fellowship as treasurer. Tanned, energetic and thriving, he also "lived by faith" (an entirely new and radical concept to me), spending a lot of time in Bible reading, Bible study, prayer and meditation.

On Saturday afternoon Vic taught me to snorkel in the clean, clear waters off Kona, notably the most unspoiled throughout the islands. I was immediately captivated by the underwater world of bubbles and coral and schools of multicolored, tropical fish.

On Saturday night he took me to the Pilgrims' open fellowship meeting in the Pilgrims' Inn, a spacious, high-ceilinged, timeworn, refurbished motel in Kainaliu, where we sat on the only chairs while dozens of hippies and former hippies with their children and babies sat on the floor. Most of the participants were not long out of the jungle and into jeans and T-shirts, yet I saw an excitement about Jesus Christ I had never seen before in all my years at church.

At the invitation to come forward for the baptism of the Holy Spirit, I again felt the urge to respond but resisted. This time my excuse was not to embarrass Vic or Gale. Or was it that I didn't want to embarrass myself?

Vic was a much changed man. He confided in me that, even after years of having taught Sunday school and being involved in other church-related activities, he had not been born again as a Christian until he received the baptism with the Holy Spirit in February 1972 in Kona. Humbly he asked my forgiveness for having failed to fulfill his part in our prenuptial agreement to establish an honest-to-goodness Christian home.

For the first time in my life, I suppose, I was speechless.

Vic confessed to being lonely. Though not praying for our reconciliation, he was praying for a mate.

I wasn't praying for reconciliation either, but I also wasn't praying for a mate. Then I remembered a teaching I had heard that, if you were divorced and the other party had not remarried, you had no alternative but to pray that God would reconcile the marriage (1 Cor. 7:10-11).

On Sunday morning I cancelled my flight to Hilo to drive with Vic across the island in his gas-guzzler Chevrolet Impala he had shipped from the mainland. We took the lower road cutting through mountains and ranges and acres of rolling, ropy fields of black lava trimmed with strings of lacy white foam at the edge of the brilliant blue Pacific. We meandered through sugarcane fields with their shady circles of monkey pod trees; through quaint towns with their idle Hawaiian cowboys and little children in sheepskin coats; and through Waimea and the Parker Ranch, the largest privately owned horse and cattle ranch in the world. Then we approached Hilo from the north with a sudden dramatic view of elegant hotel row across the bay on beautiful Banyan Drive ending near the Fish Auction House.

We met Maxine's incoming plane, then drove to Volcanoes National Park, lunched at the fabulous Volcano House buffet overlooking the enormous Kilauea Crater, then toured the fern and ohia rain forest instead of the sulfurous steam pits and volcanic calderas. After stumbling through the dark, damp Thurston Lava Tube, we returned to Hilo for dinner and the hula show at Uncle Billy's Hilo Bay Inn. Maxine was exhausted and retired to our room early.

Because Vic and I were not tired, he took me to visit a young Pilgrim couple, former flower children, who lived in a converted coffee shack in a sugarcane field. Near the end of our pleasant visit they asked if they could pray for me to receive the baptism in the Holy Spirit. Awed by the change in Vic, I consented eagerly. Whatever it was that he had, I wanted it too.

After the prayer I felt no change nor did I speak in tongues. But when I deplaned in Denver the next day, the friend who met me exclaimed, "Either you have been filled with the Holy Spirit or you have fallen in love with your husband again. Your eyes are shining."

I laughed. "Maybe a bit of both!"

On Christmas Day, Gale phoned me that Vic had suffered an almost fatal heart attack. The Pilgrims had gone immediately to pray for him.

All I knew about prayer for personal healing was secondhand, namely from the young man whose infant son was healed of croup. But I knew firsthand about heart attacks. My late husband, John, and Daddy had both had several before being felled by a big one.

I also knew that being broke, as Vic was, and not able to do anything about it would be extremely stressful. So I wrote to Vic and offered him a round-trip ticket to Denver if he wanted to recuperate in my mobile home at the trailer park. He could move into the boys' empty bedroom. But first he needed to check with a doctor whether the flight and Denver's mile-high altitude would be harmful to him in his condition.

"What will you do if he accepts?" my friend asked.

"Make sure he uses the return ticket!" was my flippant reply.

Vic came.

Our family doctor, an Episcopalian who did not believe in the "stuff Vic was into," muttered, "I know this man has a congenital heart murmur, but there's something very strange and puzzling here on my X rays."

Without commenting further he requested the EKGs from Vic's annual physicals during his four-teen-year stint with Coors.

When I delivered the EKGs, the doctor questioned me closely. "Are you sure they gave you the right file?"

"Yes," I said, "I'm sure. Why?"

"Look here," he said, pointing to Vic's latest X ray. "This heart has no murmur. It has had no infarction [tissue death that usually results from a heart attack]. This is a brand-new heart. I do not believe in miracles, so I cannot explain it, but this is not Vic's heart. This is a new, totally healthy heart, the heart of a twenty-year-old athlete."

How could this be? Vic took the news in his calm way while I was shaken. I accepted it in my head, but it was not penetrating my understanding. Even with his new heart, Vic was weak and tired easily, needing at least two weeks to recuperate.

God, who miraculously performed a complete heart transplant for Vic, kept him in Denver for another miracle, as He miraculously restored our love.

With George and Donna Loving standing up with us, we were secretly remarried — our third ceremony — on February 15, 1975, our twenty-third wedding anniversary, in the home of friends. I chose that date because it had taken Vic ten years to memorize it on our first marriage-go-round. This separation had lasted only one and a half years.

Vic offered to move back to Colorado if I preferred, but I sensed again that it would be better to join my life to his than ask him to fit his back into mine.

We told no one. Afraid to leave my job until Vic secured his contracting license and could support us, I was reluctant to tell Joe that after thirteen years I was leaving Coors. To break from my prestigious position and the prominent, influential people associated with it would be no easy transition. My one remaining finger in the political pie was my promise to Paul Weyrich that I would volunteer time and labor in his work on the congressional races a year and a half from then in the fall of 1976.

In early March I drove Vic to the West Coast to visit our boys on the first leg of his return home to Kona. The miracles continued.

While waiting for Chris and friends to meet us for dinner, we had a phone call from his base that our twenty-one-year-old son was hospitalized. In an accident Chris had fallen three floors to the ground narrowly missing a sprinkler pipe and the concrete sidewalk.

Vic was unbelievably restrained by supernatural calm, believing absolutely that Chris was unharmed by the fall.

I was frantic to leave immediately for the base hospital. Before Vic would budge, he insisted that we pray. And he prayed, thanking God confidently — presumptuously, I thought — for healing Chris in every way.

I suffered some extremely anxious moments, but when all the tests were done Chris was released from the hospital unscathed. Once again I had encountered the God of miracles.

By July Vic had obtained his contracting license. In August I drove for the last time to the West Coast, said good-bye to both boys, then shipped my new car, our household goods and me to beautiful Kona.

We moved into a cramped, hot, noisy, gecko-and-roach-ridden house that had a defrost-it-yourself refrigerator, a clean-it-yourself oven and no dishwasher. We shared it with two unrelated, former hippies, who were into health foods and unstructured lives. Even as we came to love them as our own children, I was miserable and soon bored with house-hunting dry runs, looking for something bigger, cooler, cleaner and quieter that we could afford.

Living in Hawaii was like stopping the world and getting off. On TV we got live football and canned news — half an hour in the evening, recorded especially for the islands. Chris sent me a subscription to *The Wall Street Journal,* urging me to read it cover-to-cover so I would know something of what was happening in the world since I had left it.

In early December, Vic heard from the Lord through the vision of a calendar, that December 18 was a moving day for us.

He didn't mention it to me until after someone gave us a six-foot, Norfolk-pine Christmas tree. Then he said, "Lyn, would you move into a new house before Christmas even if you had the tree up and decorated?"

"Absolutely, even if all the gifts were wrapped and the pies made," I said, "but I know it won't happen." Oh, me of little faith!

We found the house with a self-defrosting refrigerator, self-cleaning oven and dishwasher, a garage and a spare room for our business paraphernalia in lovely Sunset View Estates. We obtained a seven-month rental lease and moved in on December 18.

Gale and his lovely Japanese bride, Tsuneyo, were married on the twentieth — a beach wedding for which I made a triple-layer wedding cake for two hundred in my beautiful, new, efficient kitchen.

On the twenty-fourth we greeted guests from Coors who had come for the holidays. Our electric bill for the month looked like the national debt.

By then Vic also had a paint contractor's license and paint franchise along with his contracting license. The business had outgrown the garage and spare room, and we leased a warehouse near downtown Kailua-Kona, remodeling it to include offices, a paint store and storage. We prayerfully committed the business to the Lord, then named our company *Kana Kamalii*, which in ancient Hawaiian means children of the king. Inviting Ken Smith, founder of the Pilgrim Fellowship, to officiate, we had it publicly blessed, as is the inflexible custom in Hawaii for all new businesses.

We both believed that now, with our business in the Lord's hands, with our marriage reinstated, with renewed love in our hearts for one another, with our newfound ability to approach all problems from a spiritual perspective, our conflicts would be resolved.

So why wasn't it happening?

Because "God wasn't finished with us."

In Kona we spent most of every twenty-four hours in each other's presence, working together at *Kana K* but communicating almost entirely on family business matters and nonessentials.

Most of the time Vic was away on business either on another island or on the mainland, leaving me with total responsibility for the company. I kept books, paid bills, ordered materials, tended the store, made occasional drywall deliveries to job sites, ran errands and did everything else we had hired no one else to do, including shooing spiders and geckoes from our one and only available (and public) rest room where I also scrubbed sinks and toilets. We operated from a scanty cash flow, something I was not used to, and I was frustrated much of the time.

We had one main subject of conflict. Vic regarded Saturday night with the Pilgrims as church. I wanted to go to real church at Central Kona Union in Kealakekua because no one in the Pilgrims except

Vic was within twenty-five years of my age or within light years of my background and experience. We both dug in our heels.

I kept thinking that maybe if I could just "speak in tongues," things would change. I kept trying, singing at the top of my lungs and making all the recommended sounds. Nothing happened.

Then in August during a Full Gospel Business Men's meeting on the Nalu Terrace at the Kona Surf Hotel, Kailua-Kona, the speaker asked each of us to stand, then turn and pray for the person next to us. The person next to me was Grover Coors, one of Joe and Holly's sons, who was visiting us at the time. Grover leaned his six-foot-six frame down over my five-foot-one frame. Before he prayed a word, I started speaking in tongues and forgot all about him.

The supernatural gift of tongues helped immensely to relieve some of my spiritual frustrations but did nothing to change things between Vic and me.

In 1976, about one year after my settling in the islands, Paul Weyrich reminded me of my promise to help in his campaign.

I packed my few mainland clothes, especially the comfortable pantsuits that were still so "in" and so popular in Colorado. Just before Labor Day I left on my way to Washington, D.C., for the first time in thirty years.

I decided to spend one night on the way in Arkansas with my stepmother, Lorene, who still lived in the house where I had spent much of my childhood.

Memories crowded in on me, memories of hurts real and imagined, of misunderstandings. Suddenly I saw unforgiveness on my part become added weight to my Savior's burden as He carried my sin to the cross (1 Pet. 2:24).

Should I confess to Lorene the hangovers from my childhood? I didn't know what to do. I didn't know what to expect from her.

When I arrived, Lorene's welcome was warm and open. Even with my childhood bedroom unoccupied, she generously invited me to sleep in my father's bed in her room that night. Obviously the passing years had mellowed us both, and our visit was relaxed and loving.

From Arkansas I flew to Washington, D.C., to head up the research division at Paul's Free Congress Political Action Committee. Only incumbent congressmen have fingertip or telephone access to the Library of Congress facilities and computers. Nonincumbents, whom Paul's group helped, had no way of finding out their opponents' statements, voting records, legislation, amendments introduced and sponsored and so forth without hiring full-time researchers. Paul felt the Free Congress PAC would fill this need.

All my helpers were staffers half my age with twice my experience from conservative senators and congressmen's offices who came to work for me after working a full day on the Hill. I worked from 2:00 to 11:00 p.m., Eastern Standard Time, taking only one hour off for dinner so candidates in the Western states would have us available to them until 8:00 p.m. Pacific time.

On my first day at work Paul called me into his office and said, "I can't tell you what to wear, Carolyn, because you're a volunteer and older than I am. But I will ask you, please, not to wear trousers to work since I don't allow the young women on my staff to wear them."

I complied, of course, and struggled back into skirts and panty hose and heels.

I had not looked inside a *Congressional Record* for thirty years and was a little awed that Paul would trust me with such an important task. I also found it fascinating to be in the middle of so much excitement.

Although I was not personally involved in the presidential race, "my candidate," Ronald Reagan, was not nominated by the Republicans, and Jerry Ford lost to Jimmy Carter. We did, however, help elect many good men to both the House (Dan Quayle, for example) and Senate (Orrin Hatch, for example), many of whom are still serving there.

After the election, while still stimulated physically and mentally by the high excitement of the political arena, as soon as the Washington weather grew cold, I was ready to return home and excited at the prospect of being with Vic again. The separation had been too long.

A work increase at *Kana K* made the formerly ho-hum, humdrum job quite interesting, while sadly at the same time my relationship with Vic again disintegrated. Again, our main focus of contention centered around the same old brouhaha, church. Actually, it was only a symptom of our habitual impasse. While remaining an accommodating friend to everyone else, Vic sometimes acted toward me like an ogre. Perhaps he was too gentle to criticize me until really pressed, or perhaps I was overly sensitive. It just seemed to me that he was making up for lost time. Because we were like two unfriendly bumper cars, I shed more bitter tears during those months than ever before in my entire life.

I was lonely and painfully bored until someone

told me of an interdenominational Bible study of "older ladies" (meaning, community women who had never lived barefoot in the jungle), and I began attending their meetings. Through that association and my ensuing forever-friendships with Mary J., Mary S. and Mary M. (also known as Mimi) (to any one of whom I refer herein simply as Mary) and Jane, I was introduced to the Christian Women's Club and Women's Aglow Fellowship. Calling ourselves the "fearsome fivesome," we indulged in an hilarious eight-week cake decorating class. As a result, I made or helped make all the wedding cakes for all the marrying Pilgrims for the next seven years.

Meanwhile Mary, noticing my Eastern Star ring, took me aside to tell me that she, too, had once been a member. But when she discovered the unsavory roots of Masonry, she renounced her membership and burned her ring along with her trash at the dump.

Astounded, I questioned her more closely and discovered that, although most Masons and Eastern Star members are unaware of the facts, the original intentions in 1776 of the founders and their leader, Adam Weishaupt, were evil.[2]

As a result I removed the diamonds and destroyed the ring.

Meanwhile I kept hoping for a drastic change in my relationship with Vic. But "hope deferred makes the heart sick" (Prov. 13:12, NIV). During a weak moment of dire distress, I wrote Vic a hasty note that I was fed up and planned to return alone to Denver the next day. (Where the money for the ticket would come from, I didn't know.) I pinned the note on his bed pillow where he would find it as soon as he turned down the covers.

Being newly elected for a term as president of the Women's Aglow Fellowship on the island, I then left to preside over an evening meeting at a local hotel. When I bowed my head to pray, a wave of conviction from the Holy Spirit almost overwhelmed me. But I was trapped behind the lectern, unable to race home to remove the harsh message before Vic discovered it.

When I finally did return, I apologized profusely, but Vic never "communicated" to me whether he had read the note or not.

But God communicated to me!

In no uncertain terms He communicated to me that we both stood in desperate need of solid, Christian counseling.

SIX

TURNING POINT

And though the Lord give you the bread of adversity,
and the water of affliction, yet shall not thy
teachers be removed into a corner any more,
but thine eyes shall see thy teachers:
and thine ears shall hear a word behind thee, saying,
This is the way, walk ye in it,
when ye turn to the right hand,
and when ye turn to the left.
Isaiah 30:20-21

Spring 1978

The solid, Christian counseling available to us was just down the road at the Kona base of Youth With A Mission. The founder of the counseling ministry at the base is Dr. Bruce Thompson from New Zealand.

Dr. Bruce observed many years ago that it was virtually impossible to cure a body without also effecting a healing in the heart and soul. As a result of his observations, he left a profitable medical practice preliminary to establishing YWAM's international counseling ministry. We enrolled for family counseling sessions.

Dr. Bruce bases his counseling sessions on the diagram of a pyramid with God at the apex and the counselees at the bottom angles. The higher the counselees rise toward God, the closer they move toward each other.

The counseling had two focal points: 1) Anyone, including me, could live as a professing Christian for years and not know that accomplishments do not earn love. I had never heard that before. 2) Fulfillment comes only from the security of knowing God's love and loving Him in return. All other love relationships, including those between husband and wife and even between Christian missionaries and unbelievers, result from the overflow of that mutual, supernatural love. I had never heard that before, either.

As for point one, I had, indeed, lived my life as a professing Christian, not knowing that my many and varied accomplishments not only would not, but could not, bear the fruits of love. I had been a good cook, efficient housekeeper, competent working mother and dependable cookie jar filler. I gave more than I received at home and on the job and often felt that I deserved better. I had tried for forty years to earn love through accomplishment, striving for favor with father, boyfriends, employers, husband and sons. It never worked. I often won approbation and admiration, but no one had ever loved me for my accomplishments.

Vic often said, "Carolyn prays for something, and if God doesn't do it in twenty seconds she does it herself." I had to admit he was right. And it proved to be a hard, slow process for me to unlearn and to "let go and let God."

Whenever I had applied these principles to Vic, I realized with regret that I had consistently and uncharitably "weighed him in the balances" against my level of achievements "and found him wanting" (Dan. 5:27).

As for point two, I had to reconcile myself to the fact that God loves me — just because.

I recalled the words to a song I had heard:

> I am loved.
> I am loved.
> I can risk loving you,
> For the One who knows me best loves me most.[1]

The One who knows me best is God. If I am truly loved by God just because, then I can risk loving Vic for the same reason.

So I prayed, "Lord, is it true that You love me just because I am and not because of what I do?"

And the Lord God Almighty assured me with an overwhelming sense of His presence with the all-consuming power of His love, that He loves me simply because I am. That Vic, the husband He gave me, could love me simply because I am. That I could risk loving Vic in return, simply because he is.

At our final counseling session Dr. Bruce asked Vic, "Do you love Carolyn?"

"Always have," he said.

"Will you go to Central Kona Union Church with her?"

"Sure."

"Carolyn, do you love Vic?"

"Yes."

"Will you go to the Pilgrims' fellowship with him?"

"Of course."

It was that simple, that profound. No longer

would I compete to win my own way, no longer strive for the unconditional love found only in Jesus. I already had it.

Vic and I no longer refueled our cold war. We were just two kids hungry to know God in more intimate ways, thirsty for more teaching by godly leaders. With that in common we could go our separate ways — together.

As follow-up to the counseling sessions, we attended YWAM's January to March 1981 Crossroads Discipleship Training School at the base. We decided to live at home instead of on base, but we had two other couples from the school housed with us. To our delight one of the couples assigned to us turned out to be our old friends from Golden, Colorado, George and Donna Loving. In 1979 YWAM had acquired the M/V *Anastasis* and outfitted her for mercy ministry worldwide. By 1981 I had fallen in love with the big ship.

At the beginning of this book I told how we applied for the January to March 1982 counseling school to prepare further for serving God through YWAM in our retirement years. But God had other plans for us.

Vic went to school.

I went to Washington.

SEVEN

NEXT DOOR TO THE WHITE HOUSE

For if you keep silent at this time,
relief and deliverance shall arise
for the Jews from elsewhere...
And who knows but that you have come to
the kingdom for such a time as this?
Esther 4:14, AMP

March 1982

The summons had came from Morton Black-well, and God had said, "Onward, Christian soldier."

"Confidential assistant" is a White House euphemism for executive secretary. According to Morton, no woman who works in Washington likes to be called a secretary any more than a dealer in used fruits and vegetables likes to be called a garbage collector.

My main concern, however, was not title but wardrobe. What would I wear? During my seven years in Hawaii, skirts had lengthened, and I had broadened. Nothing in my wardrobe faintly suitable for the mainland still fit. And after seven years of bare feet, I soon decided that five minutes in high heels must be only slightly less crippling than a lifetime with the bound feet of ancient Chinese women.

On a side trip to Denver I bought whatever I could afford that went around me. Then, stocking up with six pairs of go-with-everything-beige, control-top panty hose, I was on my way, arrived a few days early and moved in temporarily with friends.

Washington, D.C., has no vagrancy laws, and my initial impression of the city was of street people everywhere, protesting everything. They even slept on the sidewalk in front of the White House. One had a jar of live cockroaches, which, I learned later, he opened and emptied during a tour of the White House public rooms.

A freak late March snowstorm hit within a few days of my arrival, catching me with no gloves, no boots, no hat, no anything to warm my tropics-thinned blood. I didn't have much money, but I was cold and found a coat I could afford at a Goodwill store: black fake fur with a white, fake-fur collar. Recalling my father's admonition, "Always dress as though you expected to meet your future boss or husband," I prayed nobody at the office or on the bus would point at me and say, "Hey, there's that coat I donated to the Goodwill!"

On April Fool's Day, 1982, I reported to the Old Executive Office Building for work at nine o'clock in the morning. I recited my name, rank and Social Security number to the guard at the gate, who then checked the information with his computer printout of approved persons. Approved, I was then escorted to Morton's office.

Morton Blackwell, from Baton Rouge, Louisiana, had been the youngest Goldwater delegate to the Republican Convention which nominated

Goldwater for president in 1964.

In 1979 he founded the Leadership Institute to train young conservatives in campaign work. He directs sessions in America, France and England and is, therefore, a hero to many young people internationally. They come to him after graduation from college or law school for help in finding entry-level jobs on Capitol Hill or in one of the agencies.

To offset his pleasant baby face, Morton wears rough, tweedy jackets and smokes a pipe.

First he introduced me, size eighteen, to Maizelle Shortley, size six, with whom I would share the office and with whom I felt instant rapport. Then he pointed out my desk and said, "There's your johnny mop and bucket."

Maizelle, the only other person on Morton's staff, was a gift to me from God. Without her I might have buckled under the weight of my new responsibilities. She seemed to know every politician in Washington and all the skeletons in their closets. And she kept me laughing with her irreverent impersonations while teaching me everything I learned the first year about procedure, especially the rudiments of typing up schedule proposals, which are requests for time on the president's schedule for our events. She also taught me to use words other than *Christian* and *conservative*, which were anathema to the schedulers.

Morton's forte is as a speaker, administrator, telephone strategist with other political activists and leader of young political hopefuls. He is not good at paperwork.

My paper trail should have been completed by April 1 when I showed up ready for work. I had done my part; I had filled out all the necessary security and civil service papers in February and sent them in ahead. None of them, however, had been touched.

As a result on my first day I had to make numerous trips (in my new, closed-toe, high-heeled, leather shoes) through the marble halls of the huge OEOB to complete the paperwork that would put me on the payroll.

Forever barefoot at heart, learning to stretch and strut (in shoes which literally shrank with every step) across the marble floors was like learning to walk all over again.

I delivered my papers to the security office, then gladly sat down to wait to have my picture taken. Security supposedly checks only as far back as your previously cleared position. Even though I was cleared as recently as 1964, for some reason they checked back to the beginning of time. And when they called my brother's wife for names of people who had known me as a child, she replied, "Good heavens, they're all dead!"

From the security office I walked to presidential personnel, where, in exchange for fingerprints and a credit check, I received a limited security badge with apologies for no parking permit. No matter: I didn't have a car.

Each time I returned to the office either Morton or Maizelle would say, "Now you have to go to...." Twice I had to go outside the building and come in again because I couldn't find my way back to the office.

Confidential assistants, though assigned to the president's staff, were actually on the payroll of one of the agencies. Supposedly that would keep the White House budget on a manageable level.

I was informed that civil service could not pay more than a set increase over a new employee's previous salary. Since I had not paid myself enough over the last few years from *Kana K* in Kona, the best Morton could do was two thousand dollars less than the minimum he had offered over the phone, with a promise of a yearly cost-of-living increase. As a result, a lot of young, inexperienced speech writers just out of college took home more than I did. Regardless, it was exciting to get a paycheck on a regular basis.

On my first day Morton took me to lunch at the executive mess, where the president's senior staff had privileges. We crossed West Executive Avenue from the OEOB into the White House and entered the basement with its deeply carpeted floors, off-white walls and halls lined with the latest photographs of Ronald and Nancy Reagan. To our immediate left was the elevator to the upstairs offices; farther down were meeting rooms, the main lobby and, eventually, the Oval Office. Straight ahead were steps down to the White House mess and situation room, also called the war room. To the right at the bottom of the stairs was the executive mess. The regular mess was to the left, a counter for food on trays, straight ahead. We entered the executive mess, a low-ceilinged, deeply carpeted, cozy room with mahogany-paneled walls and hushed tones to govern the conversation. In the center stood a large round table where senior staff gathered to share the latest in-house gossip.

We were seated and served by charming, efficient and friendly Filipinos in white mess jackets.

The food was exceptional: salads with hearts of palm, steaks, chops, lobster, vegetables steamed to perfection, homemade breads, scrumptious desserts. No bill was presented, as charges were made monthly. On the way out guests helped themselves to nuts, mints and matches bearing the presidential seal, piled in huge brandy snifters on a carved brass table in the lobby.

Because I was to be on the Interior Department payroll for a year, I was sent (on foot) two blocks away to the Interior building to introduce myself to Secretary James Watt.

When I returned to the office late in the afternoon, hardly able to shuffle my aching, blistered feet, Morton suggested we go back across West Executive Avenue to the west wing of the White House to meet his immediate boss, Elizabeth Dole, director of public liaison.

"Morton," I groaned, "my feet are screaming, and I'm too pooped. I couldn't make it even if we were going to meet President Reagan himself. And when I'm through here, I'm going to take a taxi to my bus stop."

"A taxi?" he said, surprised. "It's only two blocks."

"Yes, Morton," I said, "that's right! Two blocks!" Only later did I learn that most Washington working women wore running shoes on the street and carried their high heels in their briefcases.

During the bus ride home to Annapolis, I felt a stirring of excitement about my latest place in the "kingdom," especially from what I heard in Secretary Watt's office.

James Watt and his confidential assistant, who were among the most outspoken Christians in Washington, had shown me a recent survey by a major insurance company on the growing political clout available to the evangelicals in this country. The bottom line was that there are enough of us concerned about the moral decay in America that if we would *all* register and vote we could determine the outcome of the elections.

I meditated on the reports I had heard about the

1980 Washington for Jesus celebration, that the event not only set the stage for Ronald Reagan's election but also opened up much of Washington to Christian witness. Never before had so many people of cabinet rank and senators and representatives and department heads and others of worldly importance in Washington been so humbly willing to give their Christian testimonies. Bible studies convened throughout the city and in government agencies at lunch hours and even before work in the morning. With no chapels either in the White House or at Camp David and with job stress so high, many found it vitally important to have somewhere to go to hear the Word of God and to find someone to pray. Eventually three Bible study/prayer groups met in my White House office every week, even though I was seldom in town.

I was also gratified with the promise of a thousand-dollar administrative bonus from the Interior Department to compensate partially for my meager base salary. Suddenly, for me "the White House thing" took on its own spiritual vitality. I was humbled and thrilled to be in the middle of what God was doing in my nation's capital. I began catching the early bus to town every day to have time to scan two morning newspapers before work began.

Since I had been hired partly because of my contacts in the Christian community, it fell to me to identify the heads of all denominations and major ministries: charismatic, fundamental and evangelical Protestant, Roman Catholic and Jewish. As a result, my first week and a half was spent compiling lists and making contacts.

These leaders were then invited at their own expense to the White House for an historic event on April 13 — a briefing on the president's private sector initiatives program, followed by lunch with the president himself.

The purpose of the briefing was to urge these religious leaders to identify the needs in their communities for food, clothing, shelter and medical assistance, identify the foundations and corporations able to help, then bring the two together. This would put the churches back into their biblical role of helping the widow, the orphan and the needy, and at the same time reduce welfare rolls.

In spite of my timidity and lack of expertise, we had a very large crowd — most of the big names I had read about and watched on TV but had never met. It took some of the awe out of my job and delivered me from timidity in contacting the big wheels in my Christian world in the future.

Many of those leaders, including Pat Robertson, with CBN's Operation Blessing and "The 700 Club," returned home inspired and put into effect what President Reagan requested. Others announced to the waiting press that they believed this was the government's responsibility, not theirs.

The following weeks I boldly contacted Bill Bright, founder and president of Campus Crusade for Christ; Pat Robertson; and other such notables. I needed their opinions on the wisdom of President Reagan's announcing a constitutional amendment for school prayer on the National Day of Prayer which was coming up on the first Thursday in May. Their affirmative responses were overwhelming.

As a consequence, when it was debated in the Senate the next year, every senator received at least ten thousand calls, letters and telegrams. Several called the White House legislative liaison to report that they had changed their votes and would appreciate our calling off the lobbyists.

The amendment, however, was defeated in the Senate by only eleven votes — in spite of one of the most enthusiastic lobbying efforts ever mounted by evangelicals! All one hundred senators voted, several having flown in from presidential campaign efforts to participate.

Too little, too late? To our shame in 1962 a lone atheist, Madalyn Murray O'Hair, had already managed to get prayer removed from public schools with little or no opposition to speak of from the churches.

But out of the jaws of that defeat we snatched a victory of sorts.

Democratic Congressman Carl Dewey Perkins from Kentucky chaired a committee which had before it a bill calling for equal access for Bible study and prayer in the public schools. Young people who desired to study the Bible and participate in prayer at school during nonstudy hours would have equal access to space with those who wanted to study stamp collecting, gay rights and other extracurricular concerns. Even meeting in cars in school parking lots for prayer during lunch hours was frequently forbidden.

Because Congressman Perkins had not been able to get this bill to the floor for debate, he advised the speaker of the house, Tip O'Neill, that he was going to use a parliamentary maneuver to bring the bill to the floor after the next recess. This maneuver, which had not been used in about twenty-five years, allowed any committee chairman to call to the floor for debate any measure from his committee on the first Wednesday following a recess.

To avoid having that maneuver resurrected, Speaker O'Neill put the bill on the calendar. It passed as the Equal Access Act.

A little more than a year later, in 1984, Congressman Perkins suffered a heart attack and died. Whatever else he had done in his career, he will be well remembered by those of us who were fighting for school prayer. Who knows but that he, too, had "come to the kingdom for such a time as this."

Meanwhile in Kentucky some public schools posted the Ten Commandments on the walls in the classrooms. When the state attorney general ordered them removed, the educators had their congressman read the commandments into the *Congressional Record*. They then extracted the page, enlarged it to poster size and displayed copies of that on the walls. Not even the attorney general could order them to remove a page from the *Congressional Record*. They also made up a song sheet edged with flags and bunting with the words to such patriotic songs as "America," "America the Beautiful" and "God Bless America." I was proud of them.

Cult groups, like everyone else, have the right to come to the White House. Our president is their president, too, but they needed to know where I stood. So whenever I met with representatives of one of the cults, I would start the meeting by saying, "I believe that Jesus Christ is Himself God, that He came to earth as the only Son of God, that He died for my sins and was resurrected, and that He now sits at the right hand of God interceding for me. He is the absolute Lord of every area of my life. What do you believe?"

On the first Thursday of May 1982 President Reagan held a reception in the Rose Garden to announce the initiation of the school prayer amendment and to celebrate the reinstitution of our National Day of Prayer.

It would be my first Rose Garden affair. What should I wear? I chose a becoming gray crepe with matching shoes and felt dressed for the occasion. But a friend who dropped in disapproved of my uncoordinated hose and insisted I wait while she dash over to Garfinckel's department store nearby for gray ones. When she returned I was so pressed for time that I decided not to take time to run down to the ladies' room. I would change behind my office door. I little realized, as I was informed later, that "behind my office door" was clearly visible from the windows across the courtyard.

Instead of buying control tops, which I always wore, my friend had bought girdle top. Struggle as I did, it would not come up over my fat stomach. I jumped up and down and kicked sideways, but the waistband never quite reached the middle of my roll.

We doubled over, aching with laughter. After repairing my makeup, I barely arrived on time and wondered during the entire event if my hose were going to sag down around my ankles and the top slide down around my knees.

The Rose Garden is not large, but a platform had been erected in front of the breezeway which connects the Oval Office with the east wing. Risers in the corner next to the Oval Office portico held the network TV cameras and took up much of the space. Jerry Falwell's press people from the Moral Majority crowded in with them.

I observed the president, the first lady and Richard Halverson, chaplain of the Senate, seated on the platform, with all the big shots from TV and the pulpits and denominations of America milling around chatting as if they were at a cocktail party. In my mind's eye I saw Jesus overturning the tables in the temple, saying, "My Father's house is a house of prayer, not a marketplace" (John 2:16). But then I reminded myself that the Rose Garden is not a temple, and we had called these leaders together not for religious but for political purposes.

The event itself had somewhat of a carnival atmosphere, including a short prayer by the chaplain and a brief speech by the president, followed by lemonade and cookies served over the hedge on the south lawn. Still, it was my first Rose Garden event, and, even having to hug my hosiery with my elbows, I was thrilled to be there mingling with some of the foremost leaders of the Christian world. I'll never forget it.

Since that time a powerful national prayer committee, formed under the leadership of Vonette (Mrs. Bill) Bright of Campus Crusade for Christ, works year round to make this event meaningful in the life of America. Vonette had discovered during a study that most of the problems besetting this nation, such as school discipline and drug abuse, had exploded like mushroom clouds in 1962 when the Bible and prayer were removed from the schools. Pornography, teenage sex and abortion also ballooned with the passage of abortion on demand in 1973 in the infamous wake of *Roe v. Wade*.

When a National Day of Prayer was last resurrected from the Lincoln era during the Eisenhower administration, it did not specify a day, only that it not be held on Sunday. The Reagan administration celebrated it on the first Thursday of May; however, there was no guarantee it would always be on that day.

Vic arrived in August, having completed YWAM's family counseling school and having sold the house and business. I had already rented a condo for us in Annapolis and had started furnishing it from my favorite Goodwill resale store. At the school during a time of intercession, the Lord had shown Vic it was

His will for him to be our househusband (shopping, cooking, doing laundry and general housework) while I worked long hours under tremendous pressure in Washington. He was glad to do so, realizing that with my being gone so much of the time, he might otherwise have starved in the midst of a deteriorating house.

In December I began pushing to get the White House to issue the president's proclamation for a set date for the National Day of Prayer. By then I had come to realize that everything in the White House is done on a crisis basis, and it is difficult to persuade writers and publishers of presidential proclamations to get going in December for an event that would not happen until May.

Vonette kept calling me, and I kept after them. Without knowing for sure what day the president would proclaim, Vonette's committee could not coordinate its work to get the entire nation to celebrate on the same day.

Finally, she persuaded Congress to pass a resolution setting the first Thursday of May as National Day of Prayer each year, and thus it no longer needs a presidential proclamation yearly.

Maizelle and I maintained our sanity by keeping each other laughing, especially on the subject of diet. During these early days when I was snacking (and fretting) more than usual, a satin padlock for my refrigerator door appeared on my desk. The lock talked back whenever the door was opened and was accompanied by a picture of a hippo with the caption, "I'm not fat, just ten inches too short." I laughed till I cried.

Under the constant pressure of too much work, I wasted time and energy regretting things that were in the past, fretting about things that could be happening and, being curious, speculating about those that might happen in the future. Somehow I felt if I put in a little worry time, I could help the Lord bring things about. But the Lord reminded me that worry is sin, tantamount to saying, "God, I don't believe You can handle this, so I'll work it out someway myself without You." The "old Carolyn" was trying to rise up and take command.

Then one morning while combing my hair I could almost hear Mary reminding me, "He cares how many hairs are on your head" (Matt. 10:30).

In response I compiled a list of Scripture verses about trusting the Lord into a litany, typed them on a card and placed the card front and center in my top desk drawer. I called it my Fret List (see the entire list in appendix A). During working days I memorized the verses to help me serve God with peace of mind.

Learning not to worry really meant learning to trust that God controlled every facet of my life. As the writer of Proverbs explained, "The lot is cast into the lap, but the decision is wholly of the Lord — even the events [that seem accidental] are really ordered by Him" (Prov. 16:33, AMP).

We can do nothing to change the outcome of any event, so why worry? God-our-redeemer teaches us through our mistakes and even extricates us from the results of wrong choices that we sometimes make deliberately.

Being a confidential assistant in the White House is mostly simple serving, but everything we did had significance, especially briefings.

One type of briefing occurs when specific people, such as heads of denominations and ministries, are summoned to Washington at their own expense. They are brought into the briefing room in the OEOB where speakers from the cabinet, different bureaus or agencies spend an hour or two bringing them up-to-date on a specific subject. If subjects and audience are vital enough to our current strategy, either the president or the vice president may also be among the briefers — if his schedule permits it. Another type of briefing is held when a group already meeting in Washington requests one.

Each briefing articulates the president's programs so that grassroots supporters can understand and support them. Every presidential event, including Rose Garden receptions for Future Farmers of America or the American Legion's Girls' Nation and Boys' Nation, required talking points for the president's speech writers and briefing papers for the president himself. They all require spending time with the leaders of the groups, getting information to clear them through the secret service system and, finally, hosting special groups on behalf of the president.

One of the interesting projects I participated in at the end of 1982 and early 1983 was the Year of the Bible. This concept was originated by Bill Bright. He got the president's approval and persuaded Sen. William Armstrong, R-Colo., and Rep. Carlos Moorhead, R-Calif., to sponsor a joint resolution in Congress naming 1983 the Year of the Bible in America.

It was Dr. Bright's desire to have the president sign the proclamation implementing the joint resolution at the annual congressional prayer breakfast for the president, commonly called the President's Prayer Breakfast, which comes early in February.

Because the ACLU had brought a suit in one of the states declaring this resolution unconstitutional, it looked impossible. As Dr. Bright called to see how it stood, I agreed to keep praying that the suit would not hinder the president's signature at the breakfast. This was the first time Dr. Bright and I had worked on a project, and it was a thrill to get to know him. Prayer prevailed; the signing took place; and we became friends.

Because of my lowly position, I did not get to sit with the committee all year. Dee Jepsen and Morton Blackwell represented the White House. But I kept in close touch with them as Morton's assistant and was invited to attend their last session in early 1984 on a crucial day in my career at the White House, told about later in this book.

The White House is unquestionably the seat of power in the world's most powerful and influential nation; it is also a place of daily crises which keep everything running smoothly. Confidential assistants may not be very high up in the hierarchy, but they are extremely important in keeping the bureaucracy moving. Being a gracious host or hostess included getting guests in and out on time on a split-second schedule, while making them feel that entertaining them was the only thing you had to do that day.

As a servant in the household of the president, how little I knew what great need I would have for such Scripture verses as: "No weapon that is formed against thee shall prosper; and every tongue that shall rise against thee in judgment thou shalt condemn. This is the heritage of the servants of the Lord, and their righteousness is of me, saith the Lord" (Is. 54:17).

EIGHT

THE
WHITE HOUSE

For this I labor [unto weariness],
striving with all the superhuman energy
which He so mightily enkindles
and works within me.
Colossians 1:29, AMP

February 1983

When Elizabeth Dole, wife of Robert Dole (minority leader of the Senate), was appointed to the cabinet as secretary of transportation, a great flurry of interest arose over who should replace her as director of public liaison. The position was a direct two-way bridge between constituent groups and the president.

President Reagan's senior staff at that time was administered by a sort of triumvirate composed of Chief of Staff James Baker, presidential counselor Ed Meese and Mike Deaver, who debated, in view of the media-promoted gender gap, on who should be the token woman on the senior staff. Pressure, of course, was applied by friends and acquaintances regarding the appointment.

However, President Reagan, in late February, recalled our ambassador to Switzerland, Faith Ryan Whittlesey, to fill the vacancy left by Elizabeth. Faith is a brilliant woman, a conservative, tough political opponent twenty years younger than I, with much heavier responsibilities but much less stamina. Her social secretary, a young girl who knew little if anything about politics, Washington, D.C., or the White House, accompanied her from the American Embassy in Bern.

Elizabeth had spent most of her career in major positions in Washington, whereas Faith had served in Pennsylvania and Switzerland with no Washington experience. Faith's immediate staff, therefore, would be crucial to her success. She specifically needed an executive assistant.

White House executive assistants not only bear the same brunt of public scrutiny that their bosses bear, but they also wield a great deal of power while processing the mail and screening phone calls and callers.

Faith needed someone she could trust to handle the work load without much supervision. I was the oldest of those interviewed and had the most experience, so she offered the job to me.

I told her that Vic and I would pray about her offer, and I would let her know. Vic had just returned from the golf circuit. I was glad he was home.

Joining her staff would mean extra perks, like forsaking OEOB's marble halls for thick carpets in the White House, attending more meetings with the president and his cabinet officers and receiving both a security badge allowing entrance into any area of the White House and a permit to park near the gate.

We prayed and committed the decision to the Lord. In my quiet time the next morning the Lord gave His specific instructions through a devotion in *Streams in the Desert*: "Be thou there until I bring thee word" (Matt. 2:13).[1] The Lord was saying for now, "Bloom where you are planted."

I was glad. I loved my job with Morton, which was more people-oriented than working with Faith would be. I loved working in briefings, meetings with the president and handling Morton's correspondence. And even though Vic and I really needed the raise the full-grade promotion would command, I was content to stay until the Lord said, "Onward."

Two weeks later the offer was made again, and again we prayed. This time I felt a release from the Holy Spirit to accept. I wondered why the delay, but He never told me, and I was too busy to contemplate the reason for anything. I just studied His Word, prayed and went where He told me to go, assured that the appointment was from the Lord.

With Fret List in hand, I moved into the stress and turmoil of the White House on April Fools' Day, 1983, exactly one year after starting to work in the OEOB.

There are two ways to succeed in Washington: One way is the Lord's way; the other is the world's, which involves destroying and rewarding others on the way up. Anyone on the president's senior staff owes some political debts that can best be paid by appointments.

Following governmental protocol, Faith handed out lateral promotions (in place of pink slips) to everyone in a top-level position that would report to her except Morton and Dee Jepsen. All the other positions were left vacant.

Resumés poured in from those seeking to fill those

positions as project officers for constituencies such as labor, business, Roman Catholic affairs, Jewish affairs, Hispanic affairs and international affairs, which handled all other ethnic groups. Regardless, some of these public liaison positions were difficult to fill; for instance, the position of Hispanic liaison drew intense pressure from Cuban-Americans, Mexican-Americans and Puerto Rican-Americans and their respective congressmen and senators.

It became my job to screen the huge volume of resumés for the vacancies on her staff. It was also my job to respond on behalf of Faith to letters addressed to the president but referred to her for answers. And because Faith hesitated to hire the project officers she needed, I was soon snowed under a mountain of correspondence.

After having worked for a year under Morton almost entirely with religious leaders, suddenly I was preparing letters on labor, business, ethnic affairs, keeping up with Faith's other correspondence and serving as her personal assistant.

A normal day at the White House is ten hours. Mine usually stretched to twelve, sometimes fourteen, never long enough to catch up. Without my hour-long commute to unwind, communing with my Lord who promised never to leave me or forsake me, and dear, patient Vic at home with dinner waiting, I could have been a basket case.

Many times Faith would say, "Carolyn, I don't understand how you do it. You are here when I come in the morning, and here you are when I leave in the evening, and you always look fresh enough to do another full day's work."

At such times I assured her that my stamina was supernatural, not my own, and that all my strength and joy came from the Lord. And every time I told her, my heart reconfirmed to me how utterly dependent I was upon Jesus. Without Him I could do nothing, so why try?

Eventually she moved me out of her office into another one around the corner and hired someone else to answer the phones.

At the same time money troubles at home for Vic and me multiplied.

My thousand-dollar bonus from the Interior Department had not been cleared through the White House, and the administrator had been offended. When my papers finally caught up to him, he flatly refused the raise I had been promised, then finally compromised on half. By this time I was so overwhelmed by God's presence and His continual direction for the details of my life, I simply accepted it and said, "Thank You, Lord."

In spite of the salary, the perks were wonderful: sitting with the first lady, Faith, Mike Deaver and other staffers and deciding on who would be invited to what state dinner; meeting with women leaders from other agencies which Faith chaired and discussing how to deal with the media-generated, so-called gender gap; accompanying presidentially appointed women to Cape Canaveral as guests of the National Aeronautics and Space Administration. These all made me feel a real part of history.

Those first few months, however, were the most stressful of my entire career. Even rearing teenage boys while confronting middle age did not compare. But there was comic relief....

One day I came back from lunch to a pungent smell permeating the hallway, white foam covering the carpet and an hysterical secretary standing on her chair clinging to the wall.

"Is it dead? Is it dead?" she squealed to a workman wielding the carpet cleaner.

"What is it?" I asked.

"A cockroach!" she cried.

"Honey," I said, trying to comfort her, "you haven't seen a cockroach until you've lived in Hawaii with our Kona cruisers. They're four times the size of that little thing."

Assured that the cockroach was no longer a threat, the little secretary sat back down at her desk, but I noticed that her two feet were tucked up safely on the horizontal bars of her chair legs.

It wasn't funny, however, when I eventually started having sharp pains in the groin muscle of my right leg. I went to the White House clinic where they diagnosed a pulled muscle and treated it with pain pills and moist heat. Instead of getting better, it got worse. Eventually a CAT scan by our family doctor in Annapolis showed a cracked pelvis. By then it had fused, and there was nothing they could do for it. But how could that be? I hadn't fallen.

Meanwhile, a group of Christian high schoolers from Maryland, having been forbidden to pray in their school parking lot during lunch hour, convened publicly on the Capitol steps to attract attention to their plight. I was proud of them.

We invited the press. I tried unsuccessfully to get someone important to open their meeting in prayer. I finally gave up and went myself. Unable to get a White House car, I took a cab, had it wait, ran into the meeting, and prayed off the top of my head but from the heart. Then I left.

The next day the *Washington Post* quoted the prayer in part and, as usual, out of context.

Sam Donaldson, ABC's White House reporter, pursued Faith up the White House driveway, demanding to know if she agreed with everything I had prayed from the Capitol steps the day before.

As a result I was forbidden to pray in front of a microphone until further notice. I conceded because my voice carries well, and I rarely need a microphone. I did not quit praying in public.

One morning in August, when I had been with Faith a little more than four months, she came into my office and said, "Carolyn, Dee Jepsen is leaving her post as special assistant to the president. Did you know that?"

"I've heard the rumor," I said.

"She's leaving to campaign for her husband's re-election to the Senate. It occurred to me that you might like to have her job."

"I'm honored!" I said. "I'm surprised that you think I can handle such an assignment. But won't you be shorting your own staff by not giving such a 'goodie' to someone from the outside?"

"Don't worry about that," she said. "Would you mind not getting her title? I need that personnel slot for someone else I'm bringing in."

"No, I guess not. What title will I get?"

"Associate director of public liaison. But you will get the next special assistant slot that becomes available. You'll also get a parking permit for the south side, your White House luggage tags and executive mess privileges."

"Great," I said.

"As a matter of fact, Carolyn, I think you should move over to Dee's office right away and understudy her for the next few months before she leaves."

"Well, all right, if you think so," I said, scanning

94

the mountain of mail on my desk. "Vic and I are scheduled for our first trip to Israel for the Feast of Tabernacles in September. Should we cancel?"

"No," she said. "Take the vacation. You'll need it!"

For some reason, three Old Testament heroes came to mind, none of whom contended for the jobs God gave them to do. Moses protested that he couldn't talk (Ex. 4:10). Jeremiah claimed he was too young (Jer. 1:6). Isaiah declared that he was unclean (Is. 6:5).

I knew how they felt. Dee's job was over my head, and I knew it. But I also knew the God who had led me this far with grace and supernatural know-how in emergencies, and I was confident that He would not let me down now.

After spending a few weeks with Dee I again felt totally inadequate in more ways than in secretarial competence: Dee is tall, dark, long-legged, svelte and chic. I am short, overweight, white-haired and wrinkled. "We are the clay, and thou art the potter," I was reminded, "and we all are the work of thy hand" (Is. 64:8).

Dee speaks pearls of Christian wisdom on all subjects, both religious and secular. I speak plain talk reminiscent of high school debates and Bible lessons. Then I remembered, "Take no thought how or what ye shall speak: for it shall be given you in that same hour what ye shall speak" (Matt. 10:19).

Her clothes were elegant. Mine were adequate. Again, "Do not worry about your...body, what you will wear. Is not life...more important than clothes?" (Matt 6:25, NIV).

Regardless, I tried to convince the White House and God that I was too old. When that failed, I bought a new coat. The black and white fake fur was showing wear. In Morton's office I could hide it behind a door. Working for Faith I arrived so early and left so late, no one ever saw it anyway. I bought a Nancy Reagan-style, bright red coat.

Meanwhile, in my daily quiet times I was finding repeated references to pride: God, reminding me that He was the one who called me; He was the one who gave me Vic, the faithful foil to my impetuous nature; He was also the one who provided my clothes and, more important, the commissioning and intercessory prayers of my Christian family and friends.

"Promotion comes from the Lord," He pointed out, "and to obey is better than sacrifice. Trust Me."

Obedience does not automatically guarantee a bed of roses, as was brought home in the ensuing weeks as the old Carolyn was almost overcome with how little I was prepared — or qualified — for this promotion. Then my ever-faithful Father highlighted a verse in James during my morning reading which brought me back in line: "Humble yourselves — feeling very insignificant — in the presence of the Lord, and He will exalt you. He will lift you up and make your lives significant" (4:10, AMP).

In spite of my misgivings about the new job, Vic and I went to Israel. There we attended the Feast of Tabernacles; prayed at the Lebanese border where we could hear the shelling; danced and praised God at the Syrian border; visited the Knesset and the Wailing Wall in Old Jerusalem; marched with hundreds of Christians down the Mount of Olives with palm branches in our hands; and, finally, with four thousand Christians from forty-two nations, walked the streets of Jerusalem demonstrating peacefully for the freedom and release of Soviet Jewry.

In October I moved back to the OEOB into Dee's vacated office as associate director of public liaison to assume her responsibilities as the president's liaison with women and agriculture.

As soon as my heels hit the OEOB's marble floor, I knew by the pain that shot through my back that walking those endless halls had caused my cracked pelvis.

That night after work, suffering intense pain, I sat huddled on the curb of Pennsylvania Avenue, waiting for the walk light. It was not unusual in Washington to see a little old lady who had been mugged lying on the sidewalk with everyone else stepping over or walking around her, unseeing. But God saw me there, helpless, hugging myself, meditating on the eternal truth that God's provisions are made before we need them: air before we need to breathe, food before we need to eat, salvation before we die in our sins. And I reaffirmed that then as always it was up to Him to meet my immediate need.

He sent a man — or an angel — who helped me to my feet and escorted me across the wide and busy boulevard.

Above: Carolyn Sundseth poses with then-president Ronald Reagan for an official White House photograph.

Opposite page, top: Carolyn in her office at the White House

Opposite page, bottom: Carolyn and her husband, Vic

NINE

"REAGAN
AIDE SAYS..."

Pray also for me, that whenever I open my mouth,
words may be given me so that I will fearlessly
make known the mystery of the gospel,
for which I am an ambassador.
Ephesians 6:19-20a, NIV

For your Father knows what you need before you ask...
Ask and it will be given to you.
Matthew 6:8, 7:7, NIV

October 1983

Anne Gimenez of Rock Church, Virginia Beach, Virginia, summoned to Washington, D.C., some of the most outstanding women leaders in the evangelical/charismatic/Pentecostal world — Dede (Mrs. Pat) Robertson, Evelyn (Mrs. Oral) Roberts, Gloria (Mrs. Kenneth) Copeland, Dee (Mrs. Dick) Eastman, Joy (Mrs. Stephen) Strang, Joy (Mrs. Jim) Dawson and many, many others. The purpose of the summons was to solicit their continued support in the pro-life movement.

The gathering happened in October 1983 on the day my new assignment would be announced, which was also the day before Dee Jepsen would leave the White House for good and bequeath her seat on the speakers' platform to me.

After I helped Dee arrange a White House briefing by the president for the women, I sat in the audience. When I was introduced, the girl seated next to me gasped and jumped out of her seat. Laughing, she explained to me that seventeen months earlier a friend of a friend of a friend had given her my name to pray for, and she had been lifting me up to the throne of God in intercessory prayer every day since, without even knowing what I looked like.

At the briefing President Reagan told the women with tears in his eyes that he doubted whether such a meeting had ever before been held in the White House. He sincerely hoped it would not be the last. He told how his mother, Nelle Reagan, had instilled a love for God and God's Word in his heart when he was a child and that he had sworn the presidential oath of office with his hand on her old, worn Bible. It was opened to 2 Chronicles 7:14: "If my people, which are called by my name, shall humble themselves, and pray, and seek my face, and turn from their wicked ways; then will I hear from heaven, and will forgive their sin, and will heal their land" (2 Chron. 7:14).

In the margin next to the verse, Nelle Reagan had written, "...a wonderful verse for the healing of the nations."[1]

The president expressed his belief in the power of prayer and solicited the women's continued prayers for America and her leaders. He told us he believed that God, through His mercy, had preserved his life through the assassination attempt on March 30, 1981, and that he had dedicated his remaining days to serving Him to the best of his ability.

From this briefing arose a group of committed

women calling ourselves the International Women in Leadership. We elected a forty-member national advisory board and declared our intention to repeat the event annually.

The annual event, however, developed into fellowship and teaching meetings about four times a year. We met at hotels close to airports in such centrally located cities as Chicago, Dallas, New Orleans and Atlanta, growing to know and love each other in spite of widely diverse backgrounds, to drop masks and façades, and just be, instead of do.

Newly occupied offices in both the OEOB and the White House are often furnished with what the interior decorator has collected in her storage rooms. (It was not unusual to see two girls scooting down the marble halls in the OEOB, pushing a sofa from a vacated office before the decorator had a chance to get a hand on it.) When one is assigned to a very important post, that one is allowed to choose from the stored items and even have them reupholstered or recovered to one's taste with drapes to match. At my level, one does the best one can.

Fortunately, when I moved back to the OEOB in early September, I inherited not only Dee's huge office with its eighteen-foot high ceilings and big mahogany doors with solid brass door knobs, but also her furnishings: a couch, love seat, three easy chairs, bookcases, credenzas and a huge executive desk and chair, plus deep blue carpeting, blue walls and furniture upholstered in blue prints — very restful. I replaced two of her pictures with poster-sized prints of slides Vic had taken in Hawaii: one of the third hole at the Keauhou Country Club on Christmas Day with palm trees and the ocean in the background, the other of the hibiscus bush right outside the door of the Central Kona Union Church in Kealakekua. I hung family pictures and pictures of me with the president, with Morton and with Elizabeth, and my certificate of appointment by the president. Finally I ended up with a big space for something important, though I had no idea what it might be. I would know it when I saw it.

In early November, just eighteen months after my initial faltering steps as a confidential assistant, I was now a project officer with a confidential assistant of my own — wonderful, efficient and innovative Pat Youstra.

I had arrived at the White House believing that all Baptists were simply Baptists and that *charismatic* and *Pentecostal* were interchangeable terms.

Pat and her husband, both former professors at Bob Jones University, educated me in the fine lines separating doctrinal differences and church governments until I saw that God's children come in as many different varieties as His birds and butterflies.

Shortly after my transfer, the Republican National Committee requested through the White House that Faith speak to the Republican women of West Virginia at their gathering in Charleston, the capital. Unable to go, Faith volunteered me, and Vic agreed to go with me. He planned to stay in our fancy hotel room, order a big steak dinner sent up, watch the ball game and pray for me while I presented my first official, formal, prepared speech downstairs at the banquet. The best dress I had to wear was an ancient, faded red silk leftover from muumuu days; maybe no one would notice because it was unique.

In Charleston we checked into the hotel in time to attend an afternoon reception for the State Federation of Republican Women. After a short time I left

Vic, who was deep in conversation with someone and wanted to stay, and went back to our room to pray, to put the finishing touches to my speech and to try one more time to master my false eyelashes. But struggle as I did, one always went cockeyed and the other looked as if it might fall into my soup, so I gave it up — permanently.

While I was gone, the women invited Vic to the banquet, and he accepted.

I was stunned. It was one thing to speak to strangers whom I might never see again. It was quite another to deliver my maiden speech in front of my husband who had never heard me speak in public before. It was one thing to have him interceding for me invisibly in the background. It was quite another to have him sitting there, facing me and listening to every word.

As I prayed even harder that the Lord would guide me in my remarks and cover my mistakes, He showed me that He was using the circumstances to dig out and destroy the last vestiges of pride and competition in my relationship with Vic. I would have to grin and bear it.

As it turned out, God knew what He was doing, and I was soon very thankful that Vic had been there.

The next morning Charleston's local, liberal newspaper blatantly misquoted me: "Reagan aide calls the press un-American in her remarks about the liberation of Grenada."

I had not used that term. What I had said was that the press was upset with the White House for keeping them in the dark until after we had landed in Grenada. I pointed out that the current situation was much different from World War II days when reporters such as Ernie Pyle could be trusted not to reveal our invasion plans until such a report would not hurt us strategically.

Regardless of the fact that any leak of information now ranks as fair game for our overly competitive press, I returned to furor at the White House. Both the Associated Press and the United Press had picked up the newspaper report and were trying to reach me for an interview. For the first time I was called on the White House carpet. I thanked God that He had planted Vic in the audience to be my witness and support. I thanked Him again when I returned to my office: Someone had taped a note to my chair for me to read Psalm 54 about God's dealings with those who attack us.

That same month I was scheduled to speak to the Republican Women's Club in Maryland and to the Women's Aglow International Convention in Washington and to appear on the platform of Constitution Hall for the national Thanksgiving service. I would be seated with presidential counselor Ed Meese, who would read the presidential proclamation on Thanksgiving, and with Rabbi Ben Ami, who had planned the interfaith event and would read from the Old Testament. I would be the token woman and read from the New Testament. The token black would sing. All the men would be wearing tuxedos.

By then I was desperate for something elegant and suitable to wear.

"God, You know my budget," I prayed. "And all my fancy clothes look like Cinderella's before the advent of her fairy godmother." And there in the morning paper was an advertisement for a big sale on full-length evening dresses in a high-fashion department store in the area.

With a friend in tow, I dashed to the store. On the

half-price rack hung a full-length, basic black, designer gown with a black, sequined jacket — just my size. I took it to the clerk who said, "This one is not marked down."

"But — " was all I could say, when my friend led me by the elbow to a corner and whispered, "Do you want that dress at the sale price?"

"Yes!" I said. "It's perfect! It is absolutely *the* dress. But no way can I afford the full price."

"Listen," she said. "If God wants you to have that dress, you'll have it. You talk to the manager. I'll pray."

She prayed, and I talked to the manager. I explained that I was from the White House on my way from one engagement to another, having neither budget nor time to try on anything that was not marked way down to rock bottom. To my amazement the manager told the clerk to sell it to me at the sale price.

I thanked God who understands both my hot nature and hot stage lights. Sequined jackets are usually lined with hot, heavy satin, and this one was lined with an airy, loose, open-weave fabric.

On Thanksgiving Day the Dress made its debut under the hot lights on the platform of Constitution Hall. When the soloist sang "To God Be the Glory" my arms lifted in praise to God, with sequins flashing like a shower of tiny stars across the darkened auditorium. During the closing hymn, a few other hands could be seen raised among the vast sea of faces. I was not alone in the crowd.

As special representatives of the president, we walked a thin line, articulating the president's position on a wide range of subjects from tax reform to the liberating of Grenada, from why the president did not attend church to defense of his appointments to high positions. We had to accomplish all this in a way that would interest our listeners and win them to our point of view. At the same time, we had to be careful not to compromise our own principles. We had to please our current director and must not say anything that could be used by the media against us — a big order for a white-haired, barefoot grandmother from Hawaii who believed she was entitled to freedom of speech in a free country.

In January 1984 I served on a briefing panel for the National Religious Broadcasters at their annual convention in Washington. The topic was Christians in government.

I was unaware that reporters from the *Philadelphia Inquirer* and the *Washington Post* were among those present, while members of the NRB, supposedly supporters of the president, asked really tough questions about the president's faith, why he didn't go to church, and, if he tithed, why he didn't take it off his income tax.

I answered to the best of my ability. But the devil evidently didn't like the public platform. As I was leaving, someone called to me, "How should we pray for the president?"

Without first carefully weighing my words I answered, "Oh, for heaven's sake, pray that everyone around him either gets saved or gets out!"

The president's senior staff and my Jewish colleagues were offended, while the secular press had a heyday.

The next day after the final meeting of the committee on the Year of the Bible, to which I was invited, I returned to my office about 6:00 p.m. to find piles of notes on my desk to call both Faith and Chief of Staff

Jim Baker. I expected to be fired.

Morton called to kid me. He said, "I've never been in the chief of staff's office in all my three years at the White House. But, then, I'm careful about what I say in public."

My friend Herb Ellingwood called to say, "It would not have been so offensive if you had just said to pray that God would change their hearts or change their seats."

Faith canceled all my radio, TV and out-of-town engagements temporarily and asked me to submit for approval all future speeches on behalf of the White House until further notice.

Norman Lear of People for the American Way used my remark in his fund-raisers for a couple of years.

The Americans United for Separation of Church and State, in a mass mailing of press releases, branded me a bigot and wrote the president asking him to fire me.

One of my own denominational papers printed an editorial condemning my remark.

Walter Mondale quoted me during his 1984 presidential campaign without mentioning my name, but it did not take the press long to find me out and capitalize on it.

On the other hand, some of the Pentecostal churches made it plain that I had made them very proud.

Finally, when I made the front page of *The Wall Street Journal*, I prayed, "Lord, this has gone on too long. Was I wrong? Do You want me to repent publicly?"

And the Lord answered me through His Word: "This is good, and pleases God our Savior, who wants all men to be saved and to come to a knowledge of the truth" (1 Tim. 2:3-4, NIV).

I decided then and there that if He wanted them all saved, so did I. I never repented, but I certainly regretted stirring up all that trouble.

During a Women's Aglow Fellowship conference in Washington, Wilma Martin, Aglow's first state president in Texas, asked me if I would give a White House briefing to a small group of the women on any subject I might choose. I consented, then asked for the required list of names, addresses and Social Security numbers which would first have to be checked through a computer by the security people. An approved list would then be left with the security guard at the entrance to check the people through.

The room I reserved was on the second floor of the New Executive Office Building, which has an atrium entrance. Arriving a few minutes after the group had assembled, to my dismay I heard them already singing "in the spirit." With Christian bashing such a fad in public Washington, I dreaded what the guards might report. But as I dashed toward the door, one of them said, "We don't know who you have in there, but they sure sing like angels!"

I recapped my personal story — an ordinary woman from a small town in a remote area, called to serve as a "missionary" to the White House, twice promoted, and now God's public spokeswoman for the administration. I told them how God had guided me and provided for my every need, including the Dress, and how He protected me even from my own mistakes, such as thinking my white hair gave me carte blanche to speak my mind freely in public.

Then I made a confession. While living in Kona, Hawaii, where the best marijuana in the world is grown, sold and smoked openly, I knew of none of my Christian friends including me who were concerned with drug abuse, much less taking a stand against it. But I had become deeply concerned about drug abuse and about our deteriorating public education, about rampant abortion, about open pornography and the many other issues which were bringing our entire nation down.

"We Christians have been wonderful as lights of the world for quite a while," I said, "but as the salt of the earth, we have failed. We have abdicated our responsibility for righteous government in our country, and I challenge you to get off your blessed assurances and into your communities. Make an impact on your school boards, city councils, state legislatures and national offices. You don't realize how much one person can accomplish. That is why you don't vote.

"Most of us feel that if we establish God's righteousness and His standards in family and church, we have done our duty. But, according to evidence gathered by pollsters during the 1980 campaign, there are enough people in this country claiming to be 'born again,' that if we all registered to vote, became informed on issues and candidates, then *did* vote, we could make a tremendous difference in the way this country is run. And if we don't care, who will?

"Not only that," I said, "but we are misinformed about Congress. Most of us believe change must come from Congress and the Oval Office. Not so! Change comes in increments from the grass roots.

"I was shocked when I heard James Robison say, 'You Christians who sat in your pews and did nothing while the country went from abortion-on-demand to infanticide are as guilty of killing those babies as are the doctors and nurses.' Shocked and appalled, because I knew he was talking to me. In the early days of our country, it was taken for granted that the church would take a major stand on every issue from personal morality to slavery.

"We have been a century reaching this point of open immorality, and we will not change things overnight. But we have only to look to the early days of the settlement of the West for our examples.

"Mining towns, such as Central City, Colorado, once ablaze with saloons and bordellos [brothels], gradually became fine, moral American communities through the influence of only a few families who moved in and established schools and churches.

"For the sakes of our children and grandchildren we must make a start."

As a result of this briefing, two major changes occurred: First, God gave me a solid platform with those who love Him and were as concerned for the moral climate of America as I had become.

Second, that handful of women launched many activities to bring about change. Wilma Martin, for example, started bringing groups of people to Washington for different events such as a convention or the National Day of Prayer. They would attend a few briefings at the White House, the Capitol, the Pentagon or the hotel, where speakers in leadership positions, committed to the Lord and to accomplishing change, would field their questions. Before they left town, they would avail themselves of the Christian heritage tour of Washington. (Yes, there is such a thing.)

Greatly inspired they would return home to rally their families, their neighborhoods and their churches to action. And at the invitation of these women, I crisscrossed the nation many times speaking at churches, political meetings and Aglow chapters, repeating these principles and urging the listeners to get involved.

At the front of the room at one Aglow meeting in suburban Columbus, Ohio, stood a gorgeous, huge, red felt banner with a gold crown, gold four-inch fringe and the following Aglow motto written across it in gold letters: "Be aglow and burning with the Spirit" (Rom. 12:11, AMP).

The women came to the airport to see me off, bringing the banner with them. They insisted I take it with me.

"Will you have room for it in your office at the White House?" they asked.

"Yes," I said, "God has already provided the place for it," thinking of that curious, empty space that had been left on my wall after I had hung all my personal mementos.

It was not until June, six months after my gaffe at the NRB convention, that Faith finally risked letting me loose to speak locally and to travel and speak on behalf of the White House. We were not, however, allowed to speak or otherwise work on a presidential campaign except on our own time — regardless of the obvious fact that we were campaigning for the president's reelection every time we extolled the virtues of our administration in a speech to any group anywhere. But it was still "the rule" and not to be ignored.

When I was finally formally released, Wilma Martin arranged for a speaking tour through Texas in July. Again the pressing problem was what to wear. I packed my few cool clothes and, hoping for copious and convenient laundry facilities, left the hot and muggy Washington swamp in a cotton T-shirt, slacks and skimpy sandals. Texas would be even hotter — a dry brick oven.

Vic grabbed his golf clubs and flew with me as far as Dallas. The plan was for him to deplane during our ninety-minute stopover and for Wilma to board. My first scheduled engagement was for a "God and country" rally the next morning for pastors in San Antonio.

But as we got off the plane flashbulbs started popping from the midst of a group of gorgeously attired Texans — Reagan appointees from the Dallas-Fort Worth area — who were saying, "Welcome, Carolyn! We reserved the airport's VIP lounge so you could speak to us first before you have to leave."

What was it Daddy had said about dressing to appear in public? After this trip, even Vic saw to it that I never again wore slacks for travel while representing the White House.

Wilma responded to my request for a full schedule. She had arranged for thirty-five speeches in ten days traveling back and forth between seven cities, not including the impromptu meeting at the Dallas airport.

When Wilma and I went over the schedule together, we realized that I would be speaking at breakfast, lunch and dinner in different cities while having to change clothes between. During this time President Reagan made a trip to Austin. I was advised by Faith's office to cancel my own speech there to avoid the appearance of disregarding "the rule."

In El Paso we would be closer to L.A. than to the Texas-Louisiana border. In Tyler we would be closer to Tampa, Florida, than to El Paso. In the northwest corner of the panhandle, we would be closer to Bismarck, North Dakota, than to Brownsville on the gulf. In other words, between meetings in San Antonio, Lubbock, Dallas-Fort Worth, Corpus Christi, El Paso, Houston, McAllen-Harlingen, Tyler and Austin, we would be spending all our time either dressing, rescheduling flights, running to airports, traveling or collapsing in strange beds. Doing laundry was out of the question.

And, oh, the inadequacy of my wardrobe! Even if I could find dresses my size in the department stores, it was probable that I would meet it in size six on a plane or at a meeting. As a representative of the president, I needed designer clothes. As a representative of our bank account, I needed big discounts.

"Wilma," I said, "what shall I do?"

Wilma said, "Ordinarily I would suggest we pray, but I just saw a dress shop with plus-sizes that advertised 70 percent off."

"Where?"

"Back there!"

"Let's go!"

The driver U-turned, squealing the tires.

We dashed into the little shop and in twenty minutes bought four very becoming, mix-and-match, dress-and-jacket outfits for $144, less than 30 percent of the original cost.

And I suddenly realized that all four had been hanging there, waiting for me, just as the black, sequined ensemble had earlier.

Before I asked, the provisions had been made. My heavenly Father had *anticipated my specific need* and supplied appropriately from His storehouse.

Although it was not illegal to accept honoraria, because of Watergate it was decided that Reagan appointees would not do so nor accept any gift valued at more than one hundred dollars. But the Lord put it on the hearts of several women to contribute creatively toward my wardrobe. They put one hundred dollars each into the pot and took me shopping at the Silver Key Room of Neiman Marcus. As overweight as I was, I developed a great deal of humility standing in my slip in front of those elegant women, trying on dresses they thought would look nice on me. As a result, thanks to them, I still have some lovely clothes in my closet that I can wear anywhere at any time.

In October the National Civil Liberties Legal Foundation presented me with a plaque, which I made a place for on the wall of my office near the banner (see appendix B).

I traveled everywhere, speaking wherever there was an open door. I was interviewed on three major Christian TV networks — PTL, CBN and TBS — and on secular stations as well. At the same time househusband Vic traveled on his own at the invitation of friends and relatives (he covered eleven thousand miles in 1984) and kept our house and cars running, and our local dry cleaner busy. He also traveled with me whenever we could manage it, an added treat for us both.

But overseas travel was not in my job description, only engraved in my heart. I believe God put it there, then honored my laying it down to serve Him in Washington and across the country, first with a marvelous trip to Eastern Europe in early December 1984, with the group called Christian Response International.

CRI, active in human rights affairs worldwide is a Washington-based, tax-exempt group related to Solidarity in Zurich, Switzerland, with branches in most of the Western nations.

A core CRI group planned to accompany a congressional delegation to Ceausescu's Romania, where they would investigate alleged persecution of Christians and amass enough evidence of human rights violations to remove them from our government's trade list of most favored nations.

The group was comprised of the director, Jeff Collins; an Englishman and a Scot, both members of the British Parliament; former Rep. and Mrs. Mark Siljander from Michigan; Lynn Buzzard, head of the Christian Legal Society, from Chicago; Rev. Olen Griffing and retired Colonel and Mrs. Glenn Jones from Texas; and state representatives from Kentucky, one of whom was Tom Riner, chairman of CRI's board. With all those accents, the Romanian pastor who would interpret for us was in for fun and confusion.

When they invited me (from Arkansas) to accompany them, I jumped at the chance. But as a project officer at the White House I still had to obtain permission, even had it been for a private vacation, first from my boss Faith, then from the White House chief of staff, then from the Eastern European desks at both the National Security Council and the State Department.

Each one emphasized two things: that I make it clear I was not in Romania on official business but only as an informal representative of the president, bringing greetings to the church from him and the first lady; second, that I was to carry no literature for distribution, especially Bibles or portions thereof.

I called a young Romanian woman on the CRI staff for pointers on dressing.

"The main thing is," she said, "don't wear red."

"Why not?" I asked her. My only warm coat, my one heavy wool suit, my boots — all red!

"Because almost everything in communist countries is colorless: dull grey, brown," she said. "Nobody smiles, so nobody wears red — nobody, except 'ladies of the night.' "

I inquired of the Lord but had no leading to replace my warm, flashy red clothes.

A friend just returning from Yugoslavia phoned to warn me, "If you're going to fly in a communist plane, don't look at the tires."

"Thanks," I said. "That's like saying you'll give me a dollar if I don't think about an elephant. Now that you've warned me, what's the matter with the tires, and how am I going to *not* look at them?"

"Just keep your head up and pray," she said. "I'll pray for you, too, that you'll take off and land safely."

I packed the Dress and my red suit and wore the red coat and boots to the airport. When the men in our group saw me, they agreed among themselves not to allow me out on the streets of Romania alone.

We flew wonderful business class on Swissair from New York to Zurich, then took a communist-owned, local plane to Bucharest.

I was seated alone when an English-speaking man dropped into the seat next to me. Obviously agitated, he said, "Did you see those tires? They're bald!"

I assured him I had not looked but that prayer was sustaining us and "underneath are the everlasting arms" (Deut. 33:27).

In Bucharest we registered at the Intercontinental Hotel, the best in town, as the hub of our tour. Soon after our arrival we were warned not to ask to use the bathrooms in private homes except for dire emergencies because the plumbing was quite primitive.

The two other women in our group stayed with their husbands, of course, so I roomed alone. When we first arrived, the phones in our rooms were working. All the beds were clean with comfortable down covers and pillows. The rooms were immaculate and, surprisingly enough, sometimes heated. They were also bugged. Two men who roomed together told me that they prayed in tongues and sang hymns into their tapes, so I, too, prayed and read the Scriptures aloud and loud daily. Sometimes I returned to my room in the hotels and inns in the smaller towns across the country with their hook-and-eye locks to find the contents of my suitcase dumped on the bed. We even stayed in Dracula's castle in Transylvania, but the threat of seeing Dracula's ghost did not compare to my uneasiness about defying the communist government in their own country.

Every time the men went out (two or more at a time) for a walk or to arrange for train tickets or for whatever reason, they returned and said to me, "We saw some more ladies in red coats, and they all invited us to go home with them."

One of the young men with us went out alone the first night, which we had been warned not to do, and ended up in some security area. He was then taken to police headquarters and questioned for several hours. We all decided to obey instructions after that — to the letter.

When we returned to Bucharest at the end of the tour, our hotel phones went inexplicably dead when we dialed the U.S. Embassy number. By then the Romanian officials knew the reason for our mission and did not like it, so we had to walk to the embassy to give our report to Ambassador David Funderburk.

The only place in the embassy where we could freely talk was a lead-lined room in the attic. Even the bathrooms were bugged. (David Funderburk eventually resigned because he believed he got no support for the information he tried to give our State Department. He is now a professor at a college in North Carolina and has authored a very revealing book, *The Betrayal of America*.)

On our first day the plan was to drive some distance away from Oradeo to speak at a church site which had been bulldozed because "the government needed the lot." In truth, the congregation was growing so fast the government was afraid of it. We were not allowed to leave, however, until we had first met with the religious council of communist-approved leaders of the major denominations. Using interpreters, they detained us for hours, asking us questions to make sure we weren't a forbidden cult, preaching at us, stalling every way they could to keep us from our schedule. (Now that the Iron Curtain has fallen, cults are pouring money and literature into these countries at a much faster rate than we Christians seemingly "can afford.")

Finally, Lynn Buzzard, who had considerable experience behind the Iron Curtain, stated firmly, "We have listened long enough to the church of communism; now we will go and worship with the church of Jesus Christ."

I held my breath as the council members glared, but they let us go. The roads were slick, our drivers fast. Several times we rounded a curve to come bumper-to-tail with a herd of sheep or a donkey cart in the road. One of our men leaned toward me and whispered, "Carolyn, you ride in the front on the way back. Your hair is already white."

119

At the bulldozed site we stood on the concrete and brick rubble in a snowstorm with the largest Baptist-Pentecostal church in Europe, singing and worshipping the only true God.

The Oradeo church's pastor, Dr. Nick, had been an internist when he was called to preach. The government, angry that he had given up his medical practice for such an unworthy occupation, refused to allow his family to move to Oradeo to be with him. And, even though his congregation somehow scraped together enough money to buy him a diesel-fueled car, he still only got to see his wife and children two or three times a year.

I believe that I was the first woman to speak from the pulpits of many of the churches which still seated women on one side and men on the other. But in spite of the gloomy prediction of my Romanian advisor back home, there I found happy smiles among the Romanian Christians who risked their professions, their homes and their very lives to congregate and worship God together.

In our presence at first they were understandably self-conscious and somewhat unresponsive.

Before I stood to speak, I claimed the Scripture promise that says, "Do not worry about what to say or how to say it. At that time you will be given what to say, for it will not be you speaking, but the Spirit of your Father speaking through you" (Matt. 10:19, NIV).

I opened my mouth to speak to them, and what I said was, "I've been introduced to you as associate director, office for public liaison at the White House, but at home they call me grandma." The strain washed from their faces, and they broke into smiles.

Before we left the country (without being jailed),

we tried to convince the government to grant the workers a holiday on Christmas Day, but we did not succeed. Christmas is the same as any other day to atheistic communists.

Eventually we accomplished our mission. It had been my first trip to Europe, my first to a communist country. On the plane home we discovered that somehow, even though we had been warned not to "distribute literature," not a single Bible was left among our possessions.

We returned to America in time for Christmas, but it was the consensus, in view of how our new Romanian friends had to live, that the joy was not the same.

TEN

NOT YET, LORD?

But these things I plan won't happen right away.
Slowly, steadily, surely, the time approaches
when the vision will be fulfilled.
If it seems slow, do not despair,
for these things will surely come to pass.
Just be patient!
They will not be overdue a single day!
Habakkuk 2:3, TLB

January 1984-1985

Fret List notwithstanding, my heart's desire remained the same: to be a traveling, foreign missionary for God. Whenever I meditated on this, in my mind's eye YWAM's majestic *Anastasis* stood grandly before me, with one major complication: She still exuded no irresistible charm for Vic.

Travel with the ship was still not for me, but travel I did. And I participated in many other exciting activities I would have missed if I had bypassed this phase of my training.

January 1984: Morton Blackwell resigned his position, and I became the religious liaison. This was the beginning of my most intensive preparation.

February: "Vacation" in Hawaii. At least, it was for

Vic, who golfed on all four islands while I spoke in churches, Aglow Fellowships, Christian Women's Clubs and various other Christian groups, and also gave a political speech at a Lincoln Day luau. Of course, visiting our grandchildren and their parents was a bonus.

March: Back at the White House for many briefings. One historic one was for Jewish leaders and evangelical Christian leaders covering, among other subjects, foreign policy. World War II concentration camp survivor Shoney Braun played a beautiful love song dedicated to me on his 1620 Stradivarius.

May: Trip to Fort Lauderdale, Florida, to speak at the mother-daughter luncheon for Coral Ridge Presbyterian Church. They graciously invited Vic to come along, so we drove down through the fragrant, Southern countryside with its signs of spring. As usual, I flew back to work, and Vic took his time driving back.

June: To North Berwick, Maine, to dedicate a new church building for Pastor Bob Cole's congregation. Bob and Maddy Cole had become friends on our tour of Israel the year before. Vic stayed for a fishing trip, and I went back to work, the story of our lives at that time.

July: The hot tour of Texas already related. Also, a trip to Norway to speak at Aril Edvardsen's annual camp meeting with thousands in attendance. Vic was able to trace his Norwegian roots and visit several other European countries.

August: Guests of the PTL ministry in South Carolina with my friend Mary.

September: At a national convention of Intercessors for America, I met some of my intercessors, raised up by the Lord and faithfully standing in the gap for me.

October: Our friends Jim and Pat Carroll invited us to rest at their place on beautiful Sanibel Island off Fort Myers, Florida. In looking back, it is hard to believe that Vic got to enjoy the sand and the surf for several days, but I had to fly out after one afternoon to fulfill a speaking engagement.

November: Reunion with my family in Arkansas and a trip to the School of the Ozarks, now the College of the Ozarks, to be honored with a plaque for "meritorious achievement by one of their graduates."[1]

December: Romania, then with Vic and Nora Lam to Red China and Taiwan where I spoke in both countries in the official church and in house churches. (I did not know then how much more work I would do with the ministry of Nora Lam, a Chinese-American evangelist whose moving life story is told in the popular book and movie *China Cry.*)

On New Year's Eve in Beijing, we met the premier and were invited to a formal dinner in the Great Hall of the People near the Forbidden City. I wore the Dress. The hall was so cold that I also wore leg warmers and a borrowed mink coat.

Instead of moving through the buffet line with the rest of our group, I was tapped to represent Nora at the head table with the government officials.

The huge round table was covered by a seamless, white cotton cloth. The dishes were heavy, hotel-type china; the chopsticks, plastic. In contrast, the decorations were gorgeous: huge piles of many-colored roses carved from turnips, surrounded by wreaths of asparagus fern, and the excellent food was graciously served by waiters and waitresses wearing snowy white jackets and jet-black trousers.

After dinner the Chinese officials presented a beautifully orchestrated program for us, their honored guests, which included some of their world-famous acrobats.

Chico Holliday, a member of our group and a former Las Vegas saloon singer, had been asked to sing but warned not to sing anything religious. He had agreed, explaining to us privately that he brushes his teeth religiously but "worships and serves God in spirit and in truth." Chico, therefore, felt free to sing (with true spirit) "On the Wings of a Snow White Dove" and "Amazing Grace." The Red Chinese clapped their hands and beat on the table, keeping time with Chico's wonderful, delightful, cultural "American folk songs."

When I returned it was time to prepare for the president's inauguration. After my infamous statement at NRB the January before, this one could only get better. During the inaugural festivities I was thrilled to be seated at the head table at a brunch "In Celebration of Distinguished Women in Politics," not because of my status but simply because I had been asked to give the invocation.

The event, organized by some women from the Republican National Committee, celebrated President Reagan's bridging of the so-called gender gap. The mistress of ceremonies was Bill Lear's widow (of Lear Jet fame). Seated with her at the head table were the women from the RNC; Barbara Bush, wife of our then vice-president; three women cabinet officers; a Supreme Court justice; and our ambassador to the United Nations, Jean Kirkpatrick, who was the principal speaker. And me.

I had not sought an invitation, so why was I so

125

honored? Because God does amazing things for ordinary people who obey His call.

Immediately after the brunch, Jean spoke at a luncheon meeting that I also attended, not to sit at the head table that time, but to serve as one of the hostesses. It made no difference to me where — or even if — I sat, or what I did, as long as God was pleased for me to be there.

Did this stream of overflowing blessings just happen? No! They resulted from a supernatural, predetermined chain of events.

God, all-powerful, ever-present, knows, sees, speaks and guides. He says, "My sheep hear my voice." The pivotal word for His people is obey.

Can He be trusted with all the details incumbent upon our obedience? Absolutely! Every detail.

Throughout my sojourn in the fiery furnace of Washington, the specific detail always on my mind was what to wear. The Lord's personal, continual attention to this need, His timely and supernatural provisions — especially when considering the Dress — assured me of His abiding care over all other details of my life.

But there were times....

For instance, to go from one floor to another at PTL, one was always escorted to the proper elevator by a security guard.

I have always been paranoid about appearing on TV with a run in my stocking. In August when Mary and I visited PTL, I had just pulled on a new, untested pair of panty hose which immediately began rolling down from my waist over my fat tummy. Once again I was forced to walk knock-kneed and stiff-armed, this time next to Mary behind a PTL guard through a sumptuous white, glass and chrome office to the elevator.

As soon as Mary and I entered the elevator and the door closed behind us, I hiked up my dress and was yanking up the panty hose when she murmured, "I hope they don't have an in-house TV monitor focused on you." By the time the door opened, we were both doubled over in tears and pain from laughing.

I was to recall that incident vividly while at the New Year's banquet in Beijing. The room and I had both become very hot. After shedding the mink coat, I slipped away from the table and around the corner in the hall, then sat down to pull off the leg warmers which were making even my legs sweat. When I looked up I was completely surrounded by armed Chinese soldiers, evidently waiting to see what the American woman would take off next.

Recapping the year takes my breath away. Treasured memories like these come only from the heart of God.

"Lord, why me?" I asked.

And I think I heard Him say, "God is no man's debtor. You ain't seen nothin' yet!"

ELEVEN

FIRED UP —
AND FIRED

Pray without ceasing...Brethren, pray for us...
Pray for us, that the word of the Lord may have free course,
and be glorified...I will therefore that men pray every where...
Pray for us...Pray one for another.
1 Thessalonians 5:17,25; 2 Thessalonians 3:1; 1 Timothy 2:8;
Hebrews 13:18; James 5:16

I will guide thee with mine eye.
Psalm 32:8

God is not a vending machine. We cannot approach Him with the exact change of ten minutes of prayer, a ten-percent tithe, and ten seconds of waiting, and receive our desired goods.... God's power can't be manipulated. The all-powerful God doesn't do what we want Him to do because He has chained His power to His purposes and coupled His power with His love. Someday, when we've become all that He wants us to be, we'll look back and understand that part of His power lies in what He doesn't do."[1]

May 1986

By late spring God was stirring my nest.
The usual length of service for a political ap-

pointee to the president's staff at the level I was serving is eighteen months. Anyone striving in their own strength burns out and resigns by that time or else gets fired through a lateral promotion when a new director takes over.

Depending upon God's strength I had already served more than four years under four different directors. Many of my favorite staff members had either moved on or moved out. Briefings for different groups on the same old subjects were becoming monotonous.

I had scored a notable victory on Memorial Day, 1986, in Washington state. After participating in the five-mile March for Life, my picture hit the front page of all the Seattle papers, remarkable in that it was the first and only time anything I did got favorable media coverage.

After the march we arrived at the federal building steps in Seattle. An angry group of pro-choice and N.O.W. representatives had already congregated across the street. They chanted while resentful pickets brandished signs defending the murder of infants under the guise of civil rights.

When I stood to speak they yelled themselves hoarse, trying to disrupt my speech. They could not have known that the short, fat grandmother on the platform in the feminine, white dress with ruffles on the color and cuffs had the vocal volume of a hog caller. I had no trouble outshouting them.

One of the president's staff from Seattle informed the staff in Washington. When I arrived back home, I was greeted with cheers.

Regardless of the successes, if it was God's time for a change I didn't want to miss it.

As I was by then sixty-four years old and Vic eight

years and nine months older, we thanked God for our good health and continued energy. Then when we went to prayer we were reminded that for years we had prayed, were still praying and were getting others to pray for God to raise up righteous leadership for our country. As a result we were seeing many people putting feet to their prayers by getting involved in their precincts.

Presidential campaigns were shaping up, so Vic and I continued praying while I sent out a few feelers. We both felt in our spirits it was wasted energy.

I had offers from think tanks to work as a consultant for the usual big money when one leaves a president's staff. None was the Lord's leading for us. Then we heard a rumor that Pat Robertson might need me for his budding presidential campaign.

"Why would Pat need a liaison to the evangelical community?" I asked Vic.

"I don't know," he answered. "Maybe it's the Lord, but don't try to push any doors open. Wait!"

In July I appeared as Pat's guest on "The 700 Club" TV talk show. During a pause for the showing of a video clip, Pat said, "I understand you might be willing to leave the White House to work on my campaign if I should run for president."

"I certainly would consider it," I said, "but why would you need anyone with my limited expertise? All I do is organize prayer groups and speak to women's groups and in churches."

"That's exactly what I need you to do."

"But surely those groups would support you automatically?"

"We can't be sure. Christians are like everybody else — sometimes too easily led off track. They can promise one thing, then do something entirely different without even recognizing the discrepancies. Once I was a declared candidate, we would need an extra measure of prayer because there would be a limit to how much I could appeal to Christian groups directly."

That turned out to be a prophetic utterance. Although Jesse Jackson spoke openly of his campaign and raised money for it in the black churches across America, Pat was severely criticized, especially by the press, for his connection with the Christian community.

Later in July, Marc Nuttle, the potential campaign manager for Pat's potential campaign, interviewed me as Pat's potential surrogate speaker. I was already his intercessor.

I told Marc that if it were God's will for me to accept, I would not need a big salary but enough of an increase to show the world it was worthwhile leaving the president's staff to work for Pat. I also told him that even though I was not enamored with titles, it was important to some groups that their speakers have titles; I needed a title.

Then Marc wrote me that Pat reluctantly — but definitely — would soon be testing the waters to see if there were enough support to justify a campaign. He was reluctant because he knew his whole family would be involved, and he would have to leave CBN because it is a tax-exempt religious organization. His political strategists had figured just what states they believed he could take and that he could get enough that the momentum would carry him to the nomination. Was I willing to risk leaving the White House at that time?

I had nothing to prove and nothing to lose, and I had been involved on the periphery of politics all my life but never on the staff of a presidential campaign. So God and Vic being willing, I would be, too.

At the end of July I resigned my White House job effective September 1, asking Mari Manseng, director of public liaison at the time, not to publicize my leaving until the last minute.

I then accompanied Nora Lam on another Christian Crusade to Taipei, Manila, Hong Kong and Canton. It was difficult on that trip not to broadcast my plans, but this time by God's grace and with Vic's help I held my peace, returning for my last week at the White House wondering what my sentiments would be:

Would I regret burning my bridges?

Would I miss the perks of my job?

Would I miss the exciting people, the daily crises?

No, none of the above. I simply felt praise and thanksgiving to the Lord for helping me give my best to my four and a half years of service.

I also began to suspect there was more involved in my commissioning in Hawaii than I had realized at the time. In confirmation, in several churches and groups, strangers prophesied that the Lord had been training me at the White House for the "good works, which God hath before ordained that [I] should walk in them" (Eph. 2:10b).

My response was always, "If the White House is merely boot camp, I'll never make it in the Marines."

My final White House briefing was for a group of Pentecostal ministers. Whenever Central America was one of the subjects to be covered, I invited Lt. Col. Oliver North to be the briefer if he could make it. Such was the case on my very last briefing.

Ollie came into the briefing room while I was telling the men that their briefing was my last official act for the president of the United States. Because of his frequent appearances before a briefing room full of Christian leaders, Ollie had hundreds of people praying for him during the difficult days ahead — people he had never met personally. He gave me a holy hug and thanked me publicly for not having allowed Washington to compromise my faith.

President Reagan wrote a beautiful letter expressing his gratitude for my work on his behalf. A copy of that letter can be found in the appendix.

With no regrets I retraced the steps of my first day — this time collecting signed releases that I didn't owe any money to security, the library or the White House mess. In the archives I was invited to record on tape whatever message I wanted to leave for posterity that would later be transcribed for the record of this administration. Back in my office I collected my last few things, including the red banner from the Aglow chapter in Ohio. From outside I took a sweeping look at the OEOB and the White House, wondering fleetingly whether the prayer meetings and Bible studies that convened in my office would continue and who would speak as boldly for the Lord as He had anointed me to do there for four and a half years. Then I recalled where Paul said, "In bygone days [God] permitted the nations to go their own ways, but he never left himself without a witness; there were always his reminders" (Acts 14:16-17a, TLB).

Thus encouraged, I faced the new challenge with elation.

When I reported for duty on September 15, I was the only woman on Pat's senior staff. Because the young men at my level were earning more than I had agreed to be paid, Pat insisted that my salary immediately be increased to match theirs. Press reports to the contrary, he later appointed several women to key positions in his campaign.

We were all totally unprepared for the avalanche of criticism and general lack of support, not only from the secular media, which was expected, but also from the Christian community. I soon found out that Pat's campaign was, indeed, the Marines!

Several months before when Pat had been in Washington, he had returned early to Virginia because of threats against his life. Security was tightened.

On September 17, the 199th anniversary of the signing of the Constitution of the United States, Pat, again in Washington, tested the waters at a rally in Constitution Hall. He stated that if three million people indicated support by signing petitions for him to run, he would announce his candidacy within a year. More than three million signed.

My job at the rally was to receive VIPs on Pat's behalf because I was the only one on the staff with enough Washington experience to recognize most of them.

From then on, while at first using the campaign office in Alexandria as the hub, then later working out of our home, I traveled and surrogate-spoke for Pat as I had for President Reagan. One of the first groups I spoke to was the Ohio Women's Aglow Fellowship, and I returned the banner to them.

I still had good contacts in Alaska and Hawaii, two of the four states he won, and was able to organize early support. In Alaska I was met at the airport at 3:00 a.m. by a former Pilgrim from Kona whose enormous, three-tiered wedding cake I had made when he still lived in Hawaii. He greeted me with a lei of carnations that reached to my knees.

In Hawaii the nucleus of a committee had already arranged one meeting with pastors and Christian leaders from all the islands for the Sunday afternoon after my arrival. One from Oahu was the state president of Women's Aglow Fellowship who later organized half her island for Pat's campaign. She confessed that, when she first heard I was hired by the White House, she had thanked God for two specific things: that I was obedient when God called me into politics and that she had not been so called. She eventually represented Hawaii as a member of the Republican National Committee. During the campaign tour I met many women in other states with similar testimonies.

Christian bashing was expected from the media, all of whom insisted on referring to Pat as a televangelist instead of a talk show host. He was also ridiculed for "praying away hurricanes." While I was still on President Reagan's staff, I sat with him on the platform at a Concerned Women for America convention when CBN prayed a hurricane away from Virginia Beach. Pat told the group that all three major networks were out eagerly taking pictures of the one tree on the property that had blown down to prove damage to CBN even though they prayed.

Before Pat resigned his ordination with the Southern Baptist denomination, I checked with every major Christian leader in this country by telephone, and all agreed verbally that, considering the circumstances, it was probably a good thing for him to do. After he did so, many people criticized him on the basis that they believed preachers should not be involved in politics and certainly should not give up their ordination for elective office. This came in spite of the fact that Pat had never really served as a pastor of a congregation, although he is a seminary graduate and has spoken in many churches.

Many pastors and church leaders have been so hoodwinked by the press's insistence on separation of church and state that they are afraid even to express an opinion on a candidate or national issue. The fact is, the only thing a religious leader cannot legally do is endorse a candidate on behalf of his or her congregation. There is no reason one cannot express a personal opinion even from the pulpit.

Two things we had not factored into our plans for victory were the scandals of Jim Bakker and, subsequently, that of Jimmy Swaggart, the latter right at the crucial week before Super Tuesday.

Contributions fell dramatically. Churches that had prayed for years for righteous leadership in Washington failed to support him from the start or withdrew. They did not understand that if we could lead the economy as God would lead us, the country would not now be in debt.

When money became very tight, I was asked to give up the salary increase Pat had given me to start with, along with working a couple of months for no salary, both of which I was glad to do.

Then came Super Tuesday on March 8. At one o'clock on Wednesday morning, Herb Ellingwood phoned me to participate in a conference call with all the state and regional leaders. Pat had lost badly in the South but was still on the ballot in a number of states yet to vote. In view of the circumstances, raising money would be impossible. But we had to keep going. The question was, where to cut back? I understood at the time that all peripheral staff were fired, but the senior staff would stay.

However, late Thursday night Herb phoned again to say that the senior staff would also have to go as there was no more money for salaries.

But my omniscient Father was watching. At about that same time, I received a phone call from personnel at the OEOB, advising me that my two tours of duty working for the federal government added up to enough time to retire with a small pension. That meant that I could retire instead of resign if I submitted the proper papers along with a request within ten days.

Once again, God's timing and provision humbled and amazed me.

TWELVE

FOREIGN MISSIONS

For God's gifts and His call are irrevocable —
He never withdraws them once they are given,
and He does not change His mind
about those to whom He gives His grace
or to whom He sends His call.
Romans 11:29, AMP

March 1988

S tunned to find myself suddenly unemployed, I was unable to think what the next step should be.

Vic and I, without first praying, mulled over our options. My leaning, of course, was in favor of the YWAM Mercy Ships whose multinational crews often did a bit of liaison with government officials in whatever port they were about to enter — right up my alley. Impulsively, we decided to store our belongings at my brother's home in Arkansas first and then wait upon the Lord's leading. Meanwhile we were both drawing Social Security payments. Those checks combined with my new government pension would give us a little breather while we decided what to do. I was not ready to retire.

Even though we neglected to consult the Lord right away, He was not neglecting us.

That same night after I was informed of my unemployed status, we received a long-distance phone call from Nora Lam, whom I had accompanied on several mission trips into China. Nora Lam is a charming, Chinese-American evangelist with a great sense of humor who pokes fun at herself and her weaknesses, does not chitchat, sleeps very little, socializes very little, never goes anywhere just for fun, does not shop, fasts often and long, and spends hours daily in the Word and in prayer. Born in Beijing, abandoned in the hospital, adopted at about nine-months-old, converted in an American mission school, graduated from law school in Shanghai, and escaped a Red Chinese firing squad and a hard-labor, reeducation camp, she has taken hundreds of Americans on short-term missionary tours into China and Taiwan. Nora had heard from God. "The Holy Spirit told me you are supposed to work for me," she said.

"But I have a job, Nora," I said, not quite ready to tell anyone I thought I had just been fired.

Nora had an answer: "It is important to elect a righteous man to the presidency, but it is even more important to save the one-fifth of God's children who happen to be Chinese."

I gave her my stock reply: "Vic and I will pray about it and let you know."

When I hung up, Vic and I prayed, then both of us felt sure I should at least go to California for an interview.

Suddenly it struck me: This was an open door to foreign missions — the desire of our hearts!

I had already been to China with Nora on four

missionary trips. Each time she had put me to work, as she does all her guests, while at the same time treating us like visiting royalty. But God confirmed Nora's call with Scripture verses, signs and wonders, and soon blessed our obedience by moving us into a small condominium at The Villages, a senior citizens' golf and country club tucked away in the foothills east of San Jose, California. He also provided us with a second car which just happened to be a golf cart.

My new job title was U.S. director of outreach, Nora Lam Ministries. Again I crisscrossed the country, making new contacts and renewing old ones. Again my calling was surrogate-speaker, this time for Nora who had no time for outside speaking engagements because every year she presided over more than eighty banquets, sharing her testimony and encouraging her audiences to join her in building house churches, distributing Bibles in China and going with her on short missionary journeys into China and the Orient. Incidentally, more people are saved and healed at her banquets than are inspired to go with her.

If the White House was boot camp, and Pat's campaign the Marines, then this was the real battlefield. All the training I received in Washington, all the training in Pat Robertson's campaign, everything was being brought to bear. I saw firsthand the ravages of one nation under the god of this world (2 Cor. 4:4). I witnessed the grind and struggle of masses of people who had never known freedom: never been free in their society, never been free in their politics, never been free in their thinking, never been free in their spirits.

I realized how ill-prepared for foreign missions I had been in 1982, childishly disappointed in the

YWAM leaders and in God Himself for not accepting me right then into the counseling school in preparation for sailing away on the *Anastasis*. God saw that first I needed to grow up in His ways with His understanding of the needs of humanity, to be an asset, not a liability. And God-who-guides-me had trained me in boot camp and had trained me in the Marines and was now preparing me for war in the spirit against our spiritual enemies (Eph. 6:12).

Like other complacent Christians in my own country, I had sat on the sidelines and let the world decide who would make our laws, who would rule in our judiciary, who would occupy the White House. Like most Americans I had been brainwashed to believe falsely that our Constitution calls for separation of church and state.

It was the Soviet constitution that called for that separation. The Constitution of the United States of America most assuredly does not. Our Constitution provides freedom of religion, freedom of religious expression, freedom of religious practice. Our Constitution safeguards only against the arbitrary establishment of a compulsory state religion.

I learned that in the early days of our nation, most of our federal and local governments and all of our secondary schools and universities were run by moral people using Bible-based standards and curricula. And I learned that God's holy Word provides ample instruction in how we are to impact civil governments in our nation, in our states and in our communities — in spite of Christians' beliefs to the contrary (1 Tim. 2:1-2).

Visiting communist Romania was one thing: At least Europeans look like us. But visiting the East, especially for the first time, is a heartrending eye-opener. Accompanying Nora to mainland China, Taiwan, Bangkok, Manila and Hong Kong stretches the mind and the emotions. It is a holy privilege to pray that our Bibles and Scripture portions not be confiscated by the communist custom officials on our way in and that God confound them by giving Nora supernatural favor with their leaders.

It is humbling to carry clothing to desperate people, heartrending to find families, sometimes three and four generations together, sharing only a few tiny rooms. At the same time it is thrilling to visit house churches which Nora helped establish across the land.

It is frustrating to see these eager Christians, in their distressing circumstances but with smiles of hope, carefully tear apart the pages of the few Bibles we are able to take them in order to share even a portion of God's Word with their friends.

It is wonderful and comforting to watch how God, who knows the end from the beginning, oversees His work among us (Is. 46:10). I don't ever want to take Him for granted, ever lose sight of my complete dependence upon Him or ever underestimate the miracle of answered prayer.

In August 1989, two months after the Tiananmen Square massacre, our group of two hundred Americans and Nora's staff were scheduled to spend the night in Hong Kong, then catch the 7:00 a.m. train into China to Guangzho (Canton). There we would slip out of official meetings to visit a house church, pass out Bibles and stay to worship God with our brothers and sisters in Christ.

However, our travel agent, Nora's son Paul, came to the hotel late at night with our hundred-dollar, prepaid, nonrefundable train tickets and our visas, but Nora's visa was missing. Nora and her family agonized over it in prayer for hours then woke me around 4:00 a.m. to come and pray with them. At 4:30 they asked me to phone the White House for President Bush's current policy concerning civilian visitors to Red China.

The girl who answered the phone recognized my name because she had a friend who had attended Bible studies in my White House office, so we got our answer within five minutes: President Bush had just issued a policy requesting no nonessential civilian travel to China. Ours qualified as nonessential. Even so, we still took a vote about going into China.

The group voted unanimously to cancel even though mainland China was to have been the highlight of the entire trip. We decided instead to spend the day in prayer and fasting for the Chinese Christians and for Paul who would go alone on the train to Guangzho to cancel our luncheon and bus reservations and to greet Nora's friends who would have traveled for days across China to see her for that brief visit. We also wanted to show support for the president's policy.

Unconfirmed reports later said that the Chinese government, in order to prove to the world that rich Americans were unaffected by the June massacre, had posted video cameras at the border to record American "tourists" coming into China to sightsee and shop in defiance of the government's policy. If those cameras were rolling, they filmed Paul Lam in an otherwise empty train.

A few months later, Nora was again denied a visa, this time for her late December tour.

Because I was in D.C. at the time, I went daily to the National Security Council and to the Chinese

Embassy. Evidently unaware that God Himself had ordained Nora to minister to her homeland through her summer and winter tours, they were politely adamant in refusing to issue her a visa.

Churches prayed. People across the country who had traveled with Nora prayed. My family and I prayed.

On the Friday before Christmas, late in the afternoon, the first secretary at the Chinese Embassy phoned me to say that Beijing had reversed their position. They had issued a visa for Nora.

I said, "Good! I'll be right there to get it."

He said, "Not today. We're closing for today. Pick it up Monday morning."

"But Monday is Christmas!" I protested. "You won't be open!"

"We don't celebrate Christmas" was his sad reply. Bright and early Christmas morning, I was handed Nora's visa at the doorstep. I flew to California then to the People's Republic of China with Nora's visa in hand. The winter tour was on.

I worked with Nora for three years, often seeing her so tired from jet lag or sick from the maladies that attack those who travel abroad, that I didn't know how she could preach. But she would start out with a weak voice, leaning heavily on the lectern, then all of a sudden the anointing of God would fall on her, and she would then be shouting the message He had given her for that specific group. Without God's anointing I doubt that any of us would have anything of eternal value to say.

THIRTEEN

FULL CIRCLE
TO GO!

*Now to him who is able to do immeasurably
more than all we ask or imagine,
according to his power that is at work within us,
to him be glory in the church
and in Christ Jesus throughout all generations,
for ever and ever! Amen.
Ephesians 3:20, NIV*

November 1990

On our way home from a meeting at the Jubilee Christian Center in San Jose, apropos of nothing, Vic said, "I hope when you get this new job, Lyn, you'll have a few months off so we can go to a YWAM counseling school somewhere together."

"What new job?"

"The one that's being predicted for you."

I was amazed at this man's spiritual acumen. Several of our friends, including Nora, had indeed privately predicted a move for me, but I had been hesitant to tell Vic for fear that he would be disappointed. I should have known better. Even though Vic was thriving where we lived in San Jose — right on the golf course — he was first of all a man of prayer, and he had heard from God. He said, "I think we'll be involved with a new mission about January or February."

I thought, A new mission?! What would people our age do with a new mission?!

Nora had already told me that she believed God was moving me into a new arena, from ministering to between one and a few nations to all nations. She also believed I needed a testimony book to help launch it.

"You don't need to come into the office between trips," she said. "Go home to your computer and work on your book. The book should help you line up speaking engagements when you're traveling for the ministry."

Vic and I discussed what the new mission we were hearing our friends talk about might be. We also prayed about it together and separately. Once again we stood on the threshold of God's will but couldn't quite focus on the other side.

Then I remembered a promise I had made years before to Don Stephens, president of Mercy Ships. "Vic," I said, "while I was at the White House I promised Don Stephens that if we ever decided to work with YWAM, we'd pray about giving him first refusal on using our skills for the Mercy Ships' ministry." The ships' ministries involved world travel and included surgery, dental work, building, planting and evangelizing wherever the Lord directed.

Vic had known for more than nine years that my heart's desire had been for the Mercy Ships. By this time the ministry had obtained three oceangoing vessels, the *Anastasis*, the *Good Samaritan* and the *Pacific Ruby*, and outfitted them to pursue five basic objectives: 1) above all to make a lasting impact for the kingdom of God; 2) to raise missions awareness; 3) to procure supplies and volunteer personnel from developed nations to aid undeveloped nations; 4) to bring together as many pastors, churches and denominations as possible; 5) to develop a broad prayer and support base for current needs and for building for the future.[1]

The leaders were negotiating for a fourth ship with an ultimate goal of ten.

"What would we be doing?" Vic asked.

"Working in the offices in Lindale, Texas, I guess. What do you think, Vic?" I prodded him.

"I think I don't want to work on a ship, Lyn. I'm seventy-six years old. I quit school at fifteen to help support my mother and our family. I've worked ever since, and I'm tired of working. I'm not tired of traveling or fishing or playing golf or even running the house, but I've done all the construction work and working on ships that I want to do for the rest of my life."

I understood. I wanted to be a secretary about as much as Vic wanted to repair a ship's engine.

"Maybe you could help part-time as a consultant," I suggested. "What do you think?"

"Yeah, I think I could do that."

Confident that God was leading but not sure where we were heading, I phoned Don to ask if he was still interested in us.

"Are you kidding?" he exclaimed.

Don and the Mercy Ships' leaders and staff had discovered something: A ministry does not accomplish much by collecting supplies and volunteers from developed countries to deliver hope, healing and health to Third World countries without a firm prayer base. As a result the ships' staff and crew had been praying specifically for a liaison officer for the Mercy Ships' ministries: an ambassador-at-large. They needed someone who could travel widely and speak at churches, retreats, service clubs and women's groups; someone to expand the prayer base by representing Don and the ministry at conferences he was too busy to attend; someone to lead workshops when needed and appear for interviews on both radio and TV.

I certainly had plenty of experience doing all of that. God had uniquely prepared me through boot camp in the White House, the Marines in Pat's presidential campaign and full battle in China and the Orient. He had so broadened my field of contacts with members and leaders of the body of Christ at large that I already had friends and a platform in most states in America and in several nations of the world.

Don and Vic and I agreed to pray for either veto or confirmation from the Lord whether the liaison officer was to be me.

God soon assured Don that this was an important step for us as well as for him and the ministry. His confirmation came from the same Scripture promise God had given me many years before when Vic and I had prayed about whether I was to go to Washington at all: "You [Carolyn] have come to the kingdom for such a time as this..." (Esth. 4:14, AMP).

It is the goal of every mercy ship's staff to serve the nations they visit in such a way that they will be invited to return. It would be my goal to interest those who heard me speak on behalf of Mercy Ships enough to invite me back to share the vision with others.

I agreed to travel and speak as much as three weekends a month as long as I was not required to raise money or book my own speeches. After ironing out all the other details with Don, Vic and I moved to Lindale, Texas, on March 15, 1991, to a house in Hide-a-Way Lakes, a development with three fishing lakes and a golf course. We were also just down the road from Twin Oaks, the main North American base of YWAM.

At Twin Oaks we were introduced to the YWAM students and staff by director Leland Paris and asked to say a few words. I shared briefly about being a "missionary" at the White House as commissioned by both my home church and YWAM in Kona.

When it was Vic's turn, he stood up, pondered for a moment, then smiled at me and said, "She'd rather talk than keep house." He was inferring that he would rather keep house than talk. That suited me, too.

In May Vic and I flew across the Atlantic to visit the *Anastasis* which was moored at Rotterdam, Holland. It was tulip time, and the Dutch landscape was ablaze with color. The highlight of our week's stay was getting acquainted with the ship's crew — young professionals serving God and man, not only receiving no salary, but paying room and board for the privilege.

Many couples marry and raise their children on board. As soon as these little ones — ships' kids — are big enough to walk and talk, they evangelize in street ministry right along with the others in exotic ports all over the world. Many of the *Anastasis* staff and crew that we met in Rotterdam had been with the ship since the early paint-chipping, restoring and refurbishing days when she was first purchased.

After experiencing the ship firsthand, Vic and I returned to our home in Texas, fully confident that we had made the right move. We settled in, found a church home, circulated among our new neighbors and eased into the ministry. Vic concentrated much of his low-key evangelizing on the golf course, and I began writing my book.

In October we took a break to attend the Reagan library dedication in Simi Valley, California, an historic occasion that brought four former presidents — Richard Nixon, Gerald Ford, Jimmy Carter and Ronald Reagan — plus the present occupant of the Oval Office, George Bush, together in one place at one time.

In November we flew to Orlando, Florida, where Vic explored EPCOT Center while I joined ten thousand-plus women at the biannual Women's Aglow International conference.

Two years earlier, in November 1989, delegates from secret Aglow chapters in East Germany had traveled to America for the conference held that year in San Antonio. While they were en route, the Berlin Wall was still standing. By the time they reached Texas, the wall was down. I was sure nothing could ever approach the thrill of seeing Christian women from both Germanys, East and West, marching hand-in-hand in the procession of flags into that conference room, holding their respective flags high. But an even greater thrill came when, in the 1991 conference in Orlando, the hammer and sickle of the USSR appeared in the procession of flags for the first — and what was to be the last — time. As much as we had prayed, the crowd went wild in their praise.

Only God working through the prayers of Christians worldwide could have accomplished that, and history will prove that it is only the rustling in the mulberry trees. God is on the move. The world is in upheaval. We are confidently back on our knees, fully expecting to see flags representing at the very least mainland China, Saudi Arabia and Cuba among the new ones in the procession of flags at the next international conference in 1993.

In early December Vic and I flew to Kona to spend the Christmas holidays with Gale, Tsuneyo and their five of our ten grandchildren. While there we were blessed with the loan of a white Cadillac convertible and a gorgeously furnished condo overlooking the lazy blue Pacific to the west and the tranquil green Keahou golf course to the east, with a pale blue sky above. With no push, no pull, no muss, no fuss, we shared blessed times and occasional meals with family and friends and agreed, "[Our] cup runneth over" (Ps. 23:5c).

Even though Vic planned to stay only two weeks, I settled in with every intention of staying a full month — until I received a frantic phone call from Nora. I had promised to help whenever she needed me, knowing that she would not ask except in emergencies. She had an emergency.

Two couples who had signed up to go to China on her winter mission tour had completed most of the official papers for adopting two Chinese babies and bringing them home to America. Someone who knew how to negotiate with both the Chinese and American governments was needed to accompany them to help bring the babies out. Nora was the obvious one, but the Chinese government would no longer allow her into the country. The officials were adamant about not wanting any American Christians coming into their country to do business, teach

English or otherwise disturb the equilibrium in Red China. They were again arresting pastors and persecuting Christians — or was it *still*?

Nora was calling to ask if my schedule would allow me to go with the two couples who were willing to pay my way. I had agreed with the Mercy Ships staff to be in Lindale in early January, but I also knew by then that God seldom conforms to our time schedules or ways of doing things. I told her that Vic and I would pray, and I would call her back.

With heart and soul I had been looking forward to the two weeks after Vic returned to the mainland, leaving me to my time alone with the Lord and His creation, loafing and slowing my motor down to the roll and rhythm of the surf.

But after Vic and I prayed, we both knew that the Lord had appointed me to accompany the young, excited parents into China. On December 26, Vic flew home to Texas. I flew to Los Angeles and departed the next day for China, joining Nora's group of travelers, which included the adoptive mothers, in Hong Kong. The hopeful fathers were waiting at home.

Leaving Nora in Hong Kong, the rest of us in the group traveled into Guangzho (Canton) by train, carrying dozens of gift-wrapped contraband Bibles in our suitcases. Praying silently, we held our breath while communist border officials contemplated our baggage. Anything could happen. American Christians had been caught before with the forbidden books, detained for hours, thoroughly humiliated — even bullied and sometimes turned away. But in God's mercy, not one of our bags was inspected.

In Guangzho, while the others in the group went to see the sights, I registered us all in the China Hotel. The adoptive mothers and I soon located their two babies — beautiful, golden-skinned, round-faced girls, a nine-month-old and a toddler — with their nannies and the tour guide who had brought them down from Beijing. Leaving them in the hotel, I met the others for dinner. I was scheduled to speak that evening to the Christians at the Damizhan Church pastored by Samuel Lamb. Pastor Lamb had spent twenty years in prison during the Cultural Revolution and had recently been arrested again for his outspoken witness to the gospel of Jesus Christ. His equipment had been confiscated, and he had been ordered not to preach anymore anywhere.

The communist officials had also taken Pastor Lamb's church directory. After they contacted each family listed, warning them not to attend any more meetings, attendance rose from around nine hundred to more than eleven hundred. In the event that his church members felt it necessary to resign officially from the Communist Party and were asked their reasons why, Pastor Lamb had advised them to answer simply, "To follow Christ."

In spite of persecution, Pastor Lamb's heart still declared in the spirit of the apostle Paul, "Woe is unto me, if I preach not the gospel!" (1 Cor. 9:16).

We carried our gifts down a long, rough alley in the center of town, entered a ramshackle, old building from the ground floor, then climbed a centuries-old set of stone steps and two flights of rickety wooden stairs, each floor crowded to capacity. In flared skirt and high heels I then had to climb over a table to reach the podium. Humbled to have been invited to speak to this faithful, suffering assembly of saints, I was thrilled for the opportunity to encourage them to pray, to trust God and to support their dauntless pastor.

After the service I climbed back over the table where we presented our wrapped gifts formally, lovingly, tearfully, joyfully.

On Sunday when the rest of the group returned to Hong Kong, I stayed behind in communist China with my little brood of Chinese babies, nannies, tour guide and prospective mothers. Alone in that vast and beautiful, cryptic, inscrutable land, a little bit fearful and a great deal prayerful!

What would happen next? God had never promised me a floodlight into my future or a handbook of line-by-line instructions and descriptions of my next dozen moves, but He did promise me His Word which had always been and would continue to be "a lamp unto my feet, and a light unto my path" (Ps. 119:105).

He would be ever-present. He would never fail me.

On Monday the mothers, nannies and I got the babies up early and set off to our appointment at the American Consulate, where we filed into the building ahead of a throng of desperate Chinese ganged up outside, waiting without much hope for permission to emigrate to the United States. We expected our visit to be routine, but the bottom line was that we needed more notarized papers from Beijing before passports would be issued to the children.

Leaving China without the babies was heart-wrenching, even with assurance that all would soon be completed and approved in Beijing, and the babies released.

I was thankful on January 7 to land on American soil without further difficulty and to arrive home the next day. A few days later a woman I had met only once before, whose name, incidentally, is Mary, phoned from Wisconsin to ask me where I had been and what I had been doing between December 27 and January 7. According to Mary, every time she went to prayer during those days, God impressed upon her to pray for me. Completely unaware of my circumstances, she had simply and fervently prayed in the spirit each time until the burden was lifted. It "just happened" to be during the time of the last — the most stressful — trip into China that I have taken.

Coincidence? A coincidence is a miracle for which God decides to remain anonymous. He saw my need and sent a ram to the thicket, this time in the guise of a specific, willing intercessor for that specific, unsettling time.

🔥

155

FOURTEEN

PORTS
OF CALL

*Go ye therefore
and teach all nations.*
Matthew 28:19

January 1991

I have heard and learned by experience that short-term or long-term mission trips to China and the Orient — to anywhere — overflow with unexpected, chilling and thrilling events.

Such adventures, according to reports pouring in to the Mercy Ships base by letter, fax and eyewitness accounts, are daily fare on the *Anastasis*, *Good Samaritan* and *Pacific Ruby*.

We hear reports from all over the world of buildings built, fields planted, bodies healed, souls "delivered...from the power of darkness, and... translated...into the kingdom of his dear Son" (Col. 1:13). The stories bind together a broad range of workers — the ships' international crews, cooks, secretaries, engineers, medical and ministry staffs, "closet" and on-site intercessors, material and financial contributors — stationary and moving, visible and invisible. We are all inextricably bonded as part of a whole, all one body — the body of Christ — each member responding to his own call — praying, giving, going.

Reports come in of God's moving on hearts in behalf of the ships in unexpected ways: of tugboat and pilot fees waived as the Mercy Ships are guided to dock, longshoremen refusing payment for services rendered, berthing fees dismissed — blessings unheard of in the world of commercial shipping.

In August, while Vic and I were settling in and I began writing in earnest, the U.S. Olympic Committee chartered our *Good Samaritan* to transport the American athletes and their equipment to Cuba for the XI Pan-American Games. Not only was the *Good Samaritan* one of very few ships to sail from this country to Cuba in the last thirty years, but Fidel Castro assured YWAM's Captain Al that the crew had the liberty to go anywhere in the country to distribute tracts and Bibles. After first serving the athletes, the crew went, confident that there would be fruit from the seeds sown.

Meanwhile, in another part of the world, during the failed coup in what was the Soviet Union, the *Anastasis* was docked at Tallin, Estonia. On board ship hundreds of Christians from many nations were on their knees interceding fervently before the throne of heaven for God's perfect will to be done in Estonia, while at the same time the Estonians were being liberated after half a century tyrannized by the communist occupation.

So impressed was the crew's Estonian interpreter

157

that he and others joined the ship's family to attend a Discipleship Training School and outreach, concurrent with the ship's winter 1991 outreach to West Africa. He plans to return to his native land and hometown as a missionary for the gospel of the kingdom of God. One of the others, a woman dentist, later received a clipping from a secular Estonian magazine expressing thanks to the crew for the free medical and dental supplies and professional help and especially for bringing the good news that Jesus Christ is Lord over all the earth, including Estonia.

In spite of the blockade inside Tallin Harbor, the *Anastasis* was allowed to sail on schedule. Among the crew were, of course, sailors; medical, dental and office personnel; carpenters and helpers; electricians; plumbers; teachers; musicians and two worship teams, Lazarus and Crosstide; and ships' kids.

The ships' kids, ages six to early teens, are trained from the time they are able to walk and talk to present the gospel and Bible stories in music, pantomime and dance, to pray in private and in public, and to encourage others, especially — but not limited to — young people, to know and trust Jesus Christ, the one and only true God.

On its southward run, the *Anastasis* docked to refuel in Bordeaux, France, once the center of the slave trade to the New World. There they were thrilled to discover the mayor had organized a drive (successfully promoted by the chief advertising agency in the city) to provide the tens of thousands of gallons of fuel needed for the ship's entire West African outreach to Abidjan, Ivory Coast, and Conakry, Guinea.

According to statistics, more missionaries die from heat, insects, diseases and pestilences — victims of ruling principalities and powers of darkness — near the equator than at any other latitude. Conakry, Guinea, lies just below a short 10 degrees north of the equator.

Our leadership had some misgivings about sending the ship into a totally Muslim nation. But with the invitation of the government officials and the assurance of government approval of our activities, the trip was scheduled for early 1992. These government officials understood fully that the surgeries, dental work, buildings and other relief activities were free but were a result of our love for the Lord, and we would be evangelizing. They also understood that the relief supplies were contributed by European countries. The schools we built in the Ivory Coast and Guinea, for instance, were made possible by a sizable grant from the Swedish government for which we had applied. The hospital equipment in the Ivory Coast was a gift from the Danish government.

The ship was welcomed at the Conakry pier by a dancing, cheering crowd accompanied by an African choir wearing T-shirts with "Anastasis — Guinea for Christ!" emblazoned across the fronts.

In one village in Togo, West Africa, the teams dug wells, cleaned out cisterns, planted gardens and trained the people in how to tend them, built pens and supplied them with cows, chickens and pigs, then trained some of the natives in animal husbandry — and evangelized.

In that same village of Muslim-animists (population about 800), 650 men, women and children repented of their sins, accepted Jesus Christ as Savior and were baptized in a huge hole they themselves dug, lined with a bright blue tarpaulin and filled with water carried by their women in jugs on their heads.

159

Farther south in Abidjan, Ivory Coast (about five degrees north latitude), the *Anastasis* crew was welcomed by another cheering crowd, this one accompanied by First Lady Houphouet-Boigny who was vitally involved in our invitation to that country. Madame Houphouet-Boigny had stayed home when her husband went to Paris for a meeting in order to be on hand for our arrival, and she came to our reception for government officials.

The ship's crew took a week off for Christmas and gave the Ivory Coast a gift of a day of fasting and prayer and then exchanged gifts of a half hour of prayer for each other. On New Year's Day, Madame Houphouet-Boigny sent a thirty-six-piece band, huge bouquets of flowers and a beautifully decorated, five-foot-high cake for the crew. She was unable to come herself since she had the flu. Her sponsorship played a major role in the ready acceptance of our work in the Ivory Coast.

One of the main bridges into Abidjan had been cursed by the witch doctor, and many of the natives were afraid of it. Because public buses were not allowed on the bridge, passengers had to cross on foot, becoming easy targets for thieves.

As a result, during the first few days after dropping anchor, the ship's staff and crew waged spiritual warfare against the powers of darkness that controlled the bridge (Eph. 6:12). The battle increased in intensity as they found themselves treating wounded sailors from other ships who had been stabbed and robbed while trying to cross the bridge. Finally they stormed the spiritual gates of hell by sending their worship team, Lazarus, slowly across the bridge in a van with its windows wide open, while the members played their musical instruments and sang praises to the Lord (Matt. 16:18). Following this, the ship's chaplain led a twelve-man band of walking warriors back and forth across the bridge for an hour and a half, praying and praising God for the victory. With the spiritual enemy routed, no human enemy dared harass them. After that, the crew and staff walked freely back and forth across the bridge without harm to accomplish what God had sent them there to do.

About fifteen ships' kids, chaperoned and covered in prayer, spent a week away from the ship in the native villages and at a school for missionary kids. During those seven days they performed ten times for more than 3,200 natives and MKs and prayed with more than 150 people to accept Jesus Christ as Savior. Included among the 150 were about 15 local teenagers who, according to the latest reports, still meet regularly for Bible study. (During that same week, the ships' kids also killed a spitting cobra.)

On a Sunday afternoon, about thirty crew members, including a worship team of Ghanaians, hired a local fishing boat captain to carry them across to a nearby island to participate in a revival with a local pastor. They were armed with prayer, a sense of the Lord's presence, and their portable sound equipment. But when the sound system would not work, the team presented the gospel to the attending islanders through puppets, drama and their own testimonies. When the Ghanaian team took the stage, the crowd responded so enthusiastically that they stuffed money into the team members' pockets even during their performance. A native islander testified of his deliverance from animism and idol worship, and a Ghanaian an ex-Muslim from the ship, preached and gave his own testimony of deliverance.

The move of God obviously infuriated the enemy, but he overplayed his hand. The fishing boat captain got a better offer than his agreement with the team and stranded the missionaries on the beach. But while the team leaders bargained for replacement transportation back to the ship, the crew again preached the gospel, this time to the curious islanders who came down to the beach to see what the foreigners were up to. The enemy was routed as several more were born again into the kingdom of God. Eventually the locals delivered the team back to the *Anastasis* in increments — in their own dugout canoes.

One of the evangelism tools used in these countries is the Campus Crusade for Christ film *Jesus*. In downtown Abidjan, the crew set up a large outdoor movie screen in front of Jimmy's Barber Shop, facing the corner frequented by drug dealers and buyers coming there to "score." Thus they would be attracted to the movie and would be on hand for the Bible study to be conducted there by the crew.

A young Muslim, who heard the teaching, accepted Jesus into his heart and immediately shouted to the crowd, "You should all become Christians!" In response to his testimony, other Muslims did!

A locally known drug addict heard the former Muslim. As a result he also surrendered his life to Christ and began witnessing to his addict friends. Some of them were also converted.

One of them, a self-acclaimed dealer and pimp, had been planning to stowaway on a ship to Europe. He attended the outdoor Bible study under pressure from a friend and stayed to have his sins forgiven, throwing away his talisman and giving up smoking, drinking and carousing with women. "God is good," he said with tears. "I give my life to Him."

These reports remind me of the verse that says, "Unless a kernel of wheat falls to the ground and dies, it remains only a single seed. But if it dies, it produces many seeds" (John 12:24, NIV). Only God knows how many seeds fell during those eleven weeks in the Ivory Coast in front of Jimmy's Barber Shop and how wide the harvest spread.

Under the umbrella of continual prayer, the medical-dental staff treated 3,535 patients. They performed 201 operations (107 eye surgeries and 94 maxillofacial reconstructions), fitted 24 prostheses and filled 139 dental appointments. They saw a seven-year-old healed miraculously of an infected, poisonous snake bite that they were not equipped to treat and witnessed a fist-sized tumor disappear inexplicably from the face of a four-year-old after they had removed a sample of tissue for a biopsy.

Volunteers built a church school building in nearby Yopougan. Others constructed an operating wing on the maternity hospital in Abobo, where some seventy to eighty babies are born daily with the assistance of only two full-time midwives. With our medical missionaries' aid and irresistible encouragement (singing "Happy birthday to you!" to each baby born), many now believe, contrary to the old traditions, that "It's a girl!" is reason to rejoice. Mother and infant mortality had been quite high. If a difficult birth occurred, the mother had to take a cab to another hospital and often died en route.

At final count on the day of departure from Abidjan, more than fifty of the tough, young crowd that had been hanging out at Jimmy's Barber Shop had surrendered their hearts and lives to the Lord. Twenty-two former young toughs were baptized in water before the ship weighed anchor and sailed.

One of the most touching stories out of West Africa is that of a nine-year-old girl who was born with a badly deformed cleft lip and palate. In the village of her birth this was considered to be caused by a demon, and the parents were required to bury the child alive in a box to exorcise the demon from the village. This little girl's family fled to the nearby city rather than lose her. There they became Christians and started praying for her healing. When she was nine, a van with Texas plates pulled into the city to do medical screening for the arrival of the big white ship, the *Anastasis*, which at that time was standing at anchor in the nearby harbor. Reconstructive surgery was performed free of charge because an unknown someone somewhere, moved by the compassionate Spirit of God, had already covered expenses for that unknown child — unknown until the day when He reveals all things. Her father planned to take her back to their village as indisputable, walking, talking proof that Jesus Christ is alive and well on planet Earth.

There was one patient the medical team was unable to help who died from injuries suffered from falling out of a tree. The unfortunate man turned out to be the local witch doctor, spying on the evangelism teams. Perhaps his death convinced some of the natives that Jesus' medicine is better than his.

Togo is a nation of recurring revolutions. As a result one group of DTS students from the *Anastasis* on outreach to the interior of Togo in 1990 had to be airlifted out. Undaunted, they asked permission from YWAM's home office in Lindale, Texas, to go to the Turkish border to work with the Kurdish refugees. Once there, they were given nothing to do by the United Nations team, so they started picking up trash — by the truckload. Eventually, the U.N. team assigned them the responsibility of escorting patients from the far reaches of the camp to the clinic. In this they served so well that the U.N. has since formally requested that a YWAM team be assigned to work there permanently.

Reports come in to the base from the *Good Samaritan*: off Georgetown, Guyana, a narrow escape from a pirate ship; on the Amazon, condensation from the ship's air conditioners becomes drinking water for the thirsty crew when their supply runs out; out of Tampa Bay, the ship takes on water, but the puzzling, nonfunctioning sump pump begins pumping — after the crew prays!

Each time I return from visiting one of the ships, I am constrained to urge our sons, especially for the sake of our grandchildren, to sign up for a season to take advantage of the unique opportunities available on board: the excellent schooling, world travel and concentrated Christian training in evangelism and relationships and character building — not the least of which is learning to trust God beyond our understanding.

As the international Mercy Ships ministry is continually bathed in the love of God and the message of eternal life, and as we continually pray and seek His face and remain obedient in our calling, God continues to use Mercy Ships to meet the suffering world's cry for housing, agriculture, surgery and dental care, faithful to provide everything needed — and much, much more.

FIFTEEN

GO FOR IT!

[Jesus] told them...that they ought always
to pray and not to turn coward —
faint, lose heart and give up.
Luke 18:1, AMP

If there is anything of value I have learned during this ten-year adventure of trusting God one momentous step at a time, it is the absolute necessity for and subsequent power of prayer. Fortified and supported by prayer, to the best of my knowledge and ability I dared to take every next step He showed me and found Him in every way faithful.

Prayer is two-way conversation with God. We can pray alone, pray with a prayer partner or pray with a group, but prayer is always directed to Almighty God.

God answers prayer with both actions and words. Sometimes the answer is yes; sometimes the answer is no; sometimes the answer is wait and see. Sometimes the answer is a quiet rearrangement of circumstances and at other times a mighty crashing of walls.

Whatever His response, it is important to *believe* that God answers prayer and to stop, wait, listen and trust.

As Paul writes, "But without faith it is impossible to please and be satisfactory to Him. For whoever would come near to God must (necessarily) believe that God exists and that He is the Rewarder of those who earnestly and diligently seek Him (out)" (Heb. 11:6, AMP).

In response to the feminist movement and its emphasis on the gender gap, I urge every married Christian woman who feels God's call into ministry to pray with her own husband. When he hears from God for himself that he is to release her into whatever venture God is setting before her, then she is released. This is essential to her success and their peace of mind.

Every Christian woman who is single and called needs at the very least the accord and support of a faithful prayer partner, whether her brother, her pastor, the leader of a group or organization or simply a faithful friend. Every man in ministry needs the same. We all need someone to stand with us in the gap.

I am often asked if my retired husband, Vic, is at all disturbed by our reversal of traditional roles. The answer is no. He knows exactly who he is in the body of Christ — a child of God; where he is — seated in heavenly places with Christ Jesus; and where he's going — to be forever in His presence. I know this about Vic, too, and I never intentionally make a major move without his first hearing from the Lord for himself and then releasing me to move. He confesses to being completely comfortable in the role to which the Lord has called him, the ministry of helps

(1 Cor. 12:28).

Intercession, too, is vital. Intercessory prayer not only protected me from undue pressure from the press, but who knows what other evils might have tripped me up had I not been lifted before the throne of God by many willing intercessors. Sometimes I would phone an intercessor to say I was going into the lions' den and needed the mouths of the lions to be shut. That is all they needed to know to stand effectually in the gap.

"Men may spurn our appeals, reject our message, oppose our arguments, despise our persons, but they are helpless against our prayers," said J. Sidlow Baxter.[1] My advice, then, is this: Worship, praise and pray without ceasing. It is never too late to begin. When all else fails (and without prayer it will), pray. Then go for it!

But does God have a plan for everyone's life? Yes! Vic and I are living proof that He who works all things together for good to give us the desires of our hearts is no respecter of persons (Acts 10:34). He does not search for the young, beautiful, slender, talented, wealthy, experienced, courageous, worldly wise, well equipped or those who know how to defend themselves. Rather He searches for the humble and willing like Isaiah, those who simply say, "Here am I; send me" (Is. 6:8c).

We are never too young or too old, never too fat or too thin, never too rich or too poor to obey God.

With what abandon we would serve Him if we could only know the end from the beginning — or so we think! In my case, I'm not at all sure how abandoned to His will I would have been, had He shown me at age sixty how He would train me for my present job with Mercy Ships: I would first have to travel so many thousands of miles, speak at so many hundreds of meetings in so many states and nations to so many hundreds of thousands of people. And I would first be persecuted so many times by the media and by government red tape and fret so many times over what to wear while representing not only my president, but also my King.

Fretting never once supplied my needs. The key to an abundant supply is so simple that we often miss it: "Seek ye first the kingdom of God, and His righteousness; and all these things shall be added unto you" (Matt. 6:33).

God in His wisdom never allowed me to jump ahead of Him. He always trained me ahead of time in specific ways for what was to follow, constantly confirming His attention to detail by supplying not sparingly, but generously, everything needed to accomplish and embellish His unique call on my life. He gave me exceptional stamina and energy for someone my age, the gift of gab, advocacy in strategic places, the always appropriate wardrobe as exemplified by the Dress, and best of all, a wonderful, supportive prayer partner in the person of my husband, Vic.

And intercessors. Concrete evidence of the power of their intercession is that, aside from the media harassment, I was never again called on the White House carpet.

By all these gifts and signs and wonders, God greatly expanded my horizons and reinforced my faith. Launching out on my own I would surely have failed from just plain burnout, sheer energy expended through trying to supply for my needs in my own strength.

Fearing to follow God is from the enemy. We need

never be intimidated by His call. "For God did not give us a spirit of timidity...but...of power and of love and of calm and well-balanced mind and discipline and self-control" (2 Tim. 1:7, AMP).

Obedience never ends in lack. Sheila Walsh, co-host of "The 700 Club" talk show, writes: "Our hope in Christ enables us to come to God with open hands into which He can place what He wants and out of which He can take what should not be there."[2]

We are His ambassadors, representing the King of kings and the Lord of lords at work, at play, in the home, in the neighborhood, in the church, on the mission field.

Every aspect of our enablement to fulfill His call, whether "Onward, Christian soldiers," or "Bloom where you're planted," reflects on Him and on His provisions. We are all children of the Father. "He who did not withhold or spare [even] His own Son but gave Him up for us all, will He not also with Him freely and graciously give us all [other] things?" (Rom. 8:32, AMP).

Who can imagine what is next on God's agenda for us grandparents? Even though Vic and I have a combined age of 147 years, God has not finished with us. Because we know our God, we have confidence that what is to come will be the best yet.

He has a thicket in place and a ram coming up the mountain. Therefore, where He leads, we will follow.

We urge you to do the same so that you, too, can rejoice and sing from the heart: "I run in the path of your commands, for you have set my heart free" (Ps. 119:32, NIV).

FRET LIST

Roll your works upon the Lord — commit and trust them wholly to Him; [He will cause your thoughts to become agreeable to His will, and] so shall your plans be established and succeed (Prov. 16:3, AMP).

Do not fret because of evil men or be envious of those who do wrong; for like the grass they will soon wither, like green plants they will soon die away (Ps. 37:1-2, NIV).

Commit your way to the Lord; trust in him and he will do this: He will make your righteousness shine like the dawn, the justice of your cause like the noonday sun (Ps. 37:5-6, NIV).

Do not fret when men succeed in their ways, when they carry out their wicked schemes. Refrain from anger and turn from wrath; do not fret — it leads only to evil. For evil men will be cut off, but those who hope in the Lord will inherit the land (Ps. 37:7b-8, NIV).

Humble yourselves, therefore, under God's mighty hand, that he may lift you up in due time. Cast all your anxiety on him because he cares for you (1 Pet. 5:6-7, NIV).

Therefore I tell you, do not worry...look at the birds of the air...are you not more valuable than they? Who of you by worrying can add a single hour to his life?...But seek first his kingdom and his righteousness and all these things will be given to you as well. Therefore do not worry about tomorrow, for tomorrow will worry about itself. Each day has enough trouble of its own (Matt. 6:25-27, 33-34, NIV).

APPENDIX B

*Text of the plaque given to Carolyn Sundseth
on October 30, 1984, by the National Civil
Liberties Legal Foundation Inc.*

Promoting understanding and
communication between Americans
and their leaders is
what keeps our country free.

As Associate Director,
Office for Public Liaison at the White House,
CAROLYN SUNDSETH
has brought together national leaders
and diverse groups of people
from all walks of life
for the purpose of understanding
and communicating
the great issues of our time.
Of all the great issues that face modern man,
none is more critical than civil liberty.

Through the outstanding efforts of
CAROLYN SUNDSETH,
many Americans can learn from their leaders
the priceless value of civil liberties.
And from the people they serve,
America's leaders can learn
to guard those civil liberties well.
Because her activities have strengthened

our personal freedoms,
NATIONAL CIVIL LIBERTIES
LEGAL FOUNDATION
wishes to honor

CAROLYN SUNDSETH:
SPECIAL ADVOCATE OF CIVIL LIBERTIES

An advocate is one who pleads
the cause of another.
This title is not acknowledgement
nor decoration. It is not praise nor reward.
Neither in its deepest sense,
is it mere honor. It is, rather,
a somber recognition of the price paid
by those who choose to beget liberty
and to bestow its blessings upon others,
rather than to enjoy those blessings themselves.
For throughout time,
the truly great have spent
their own lives and interests
to purchase for others the blessings and fruits
of freedom which they themselves
may rarely share.

Those who founded this nation
pledged to it their lives, their fortunes,
and their sacred honor.
But of those giants who covenanted,
few were left alive or unravaged
to author the Constitution
which secured to their posterity
the blessings of that liberty
for which they suffered.

174

Advocates, therefore,
may not enjoy liberty as others enjoy it.
Their liberty is no pleasure if others still suffer.
If there be not justice for the many,
then freedom holds little comfort for the few.

Advocates may not live as others live.
They vow to beget and bestow.
It is no light vow.
It carries the price of sobriety, of exhaustion,
of suffering, and of burdens
that few can understand
and that fewer can bear.
It is a vow that only the great,
touched by the God of Providence,
can comprehend or make.

Once an advocate,
you may never again live unto yourself.
You must live unto your fellow man.
Above all, you must live unto your God.

Greater love hath no man than this,
that a man lay down his life for his friends.
John 15:13

APPENDIX C

THE WHITE HOUSE
WASHINGTON

Santa Barbara

August 25, 1986

Dear Carolyn:

On your departure from the White House, I want to thank you for your selfless dedication and untiring efforts on my behalf in the Office of Public Liaison for the past four and a half years.

Your enthusiasm and resourcefulness in reaching out to religious groups, making sure that they had a sympathetic ear in this Administration, were of invaluable assistance in responding to their needs and in winning support for our agenda.

You were always willing to add to your crowded days, not to mention evenings and weekends, one more call, one more meeting, another speaking engagement or a last-minute reception — all to ensure that no opportunity was lost in getting our message across and in showing how much this Administration appreciates the good that our religious institutions bring to this great nation.

Carolyn, I counted on you and you made more friends for me than I'll ever be able to count. I will always be in your debt. But you are that rare person who loves the work more than the reward. In fact, that's the secret of your success — that and an abundance of energy, cheerfulness, and kindness. Perhaps these last three traits are your reward for giving unselfishly of yourself to a worthwhile cause.

Again, thank you. Nancy and I ask God's richest blessings on you, Vic, and your family and on all your future endeavors.

Sincerely,

Ronald Reagan

Mrs. Carolyn B. Sundseth
The White House
Washington, D.C.

NOTES

Chapter 1

1. For more details about that exciting story see Loren Cunningham and Janice Rogers, *Is That Really You, God?* (Old Tappan, N.J.: Fleming H. Revell, 1984).

2. Oswald Chambers, *My Utmost for His Highest* (New York: Dodd, Mead & Company, 1957), p. 268.

Chapter 2

1. See William T. Still, *New World Order: The Ancient Plan of Secret Society* (Lafayette, La.: Huntington House, 1990), or E.M. Storms, *Should a Christian Be a Mason?* (Fletcher, N.C.: New Puritan Library, 1987).

Chapter 5

1. John Sherrill, *They Speak With Other Tongues* (Old Tappan, N.J.: Fleming H. Revell, Chosen, 1979).

2. See Still, *New World Order*, or Storms, *Should a Christian Be a Mason?*

Chapter 6

1. "I Am Loved." Words by William J. and Gloria Gaither. Music by William J. Gaither. Copyright © by William J. Gaither. All rights reserved. Used by permission.

Chapter 8

1. Mrs. Charles E. Cowman, *Streams in the Desert* (Grand Rapids, Mich.: Zondervan, 1984). This devotional was first published in 1925.

Chapter 9

1. This story was distributed by the Associated Press in January 1980.

Chapter 10

1. The plaque from the School of the Ozarks read: Alumni Association Meritorious Achievement Award presented to Carolyn (Brown) Sundseth for continuing interest and loyalty to the School of the Ozarks, Christian living, community service and personal achievement.

Chapter 11

1. Eliza Morgan, "The Attributes of God: Omnipotent," *Moody Monthly*, January 1986, p. 31.

Chapter 13

1. Don Stephens, "Pick-A-Port," *Mercy Ships*, August 1991, p. 6. *Mercy Ships* is a newsletter published by Youth With A Mission in Lindale, Texas.

Chapter 15

1. This quote was copied from a National Day of Prayer flyer, where it was credited to J. Sidlow Baxter.

2. Sheila Walsh, *Holding Onto Heaven With Hell on Your Back* (Nashville, Tenn.: Thomas Nelson, 1990), p. 75.

Carolyn Sundseth is an outstanding motivational speaker. Whether she's sharing exciting testimonies from Mercy Ship outreaches, God's dealings in her own life or foundational truths from the Word, her energy is boundless, and her love for the Lord is contagious.

To book Carolyn Sundseth for your church, conference, Christian Women's Club, Women's Aglow Fellowship, civic club or other group, please write or call:

Motivational Speaker

Mrs. Carolyn Sundseth
1186 Escondido Dr.
Sierra Vista, AZ 85635-8204

vic-carolyn@sundseth.com

Phone: (520) 459-7504

WHAT ENTHUSIASTIC AUDIENCES SAY ABOUT CAROLYN SUNDSETH

"We could listen to you for hours.
Don't quit now!"

"Today I heard Mercy Ships liaison officer
Carolyn Sundseth. She is a beautiful
representative of your ministry,
and she really lit my fire, and that of my wife,
for world missions."

"Carolyn, you are a delight;
you have touched and left your mark
upon us. You are one
of those conference speakers we
will be talking about for years to come."

"I found Carolyn's views timely,
insightful and of extreme importance
to Christians in America.
She's a treasure and a gift
to the Christian community."

"...it was an hour of side-splitting laughter
and profound spiritual truth.
Carolyn Sundseth's teaching has
revolutionized my prayer life."